Realizing Gender Equality in Higher Education:
The Need to Integrate Work/Family Issues

by Nancy Hensel

ASHE-ERIC Higher Education Report 2, 1991

Prepared by

Clearinghouse on Higher Education
The George Washington University

In cooperation with

Association for the Study
of Higher Education

Published by

School of Education and Human Development
The George Washington University

Jonathan D. Fife, Series Editor

Cite as
Hensel, Nancy. 1991. *Realizing Gender Equality in Higher Education: The Need to Integrate Work/Family Issues.* ASHE-ERIC Higher Education Report No. 2. Washington, D.C.: The George Washington University, School of Education and Human Development.

Library of Congress Catalog Card Number 91-66411
ISSN 0884-0040
ISBN 1-878380-07-9

Managing Editor: Bryan Hollister
Manuscript Editor: Katharine Bird
Cover design by Michael David Brown, Rockville, Maryland

The ERIC Clearinghouse on Higher Education invites individuals to submit proposals for writing monographs for the *ASHE-ERIC Higher Education Report* series. Proposals must include:
1. A detailed manuscript proposal of not more than five pages.
2. A chapter-by-chapter outline.
3. A 75-word summary to be used by several review committees for the initial screening and rating of each proposal.
4. A vita and a writing sample.

ERIC Clearinghouse on Higher Education
School of Education and Human Development
The George Washington University
One Dupont Circle, Suite 630
Washington, DC 20036-1183

This publication was prepared partially with funding from the Office of Educational Research and Improvement, U.S. Department of Education, under contract no. ED RI-88-062014. The opinions expressed in this report do not necessarily reflect the positions or policies of OERI or the Department.

EXECUTIVE SUMMARY

American higher education is facing a severe shortage of qualified teachers at the same time that it is under pressure to diversify its faculties. Colleges and universities must recruit an estimated 335,000 new faculty to meet needs in the next decade, and yet declining enrollments at the nation's graduate institutions suggest that those with doctorates will be in short supply. Qualified minorities will be even scarcer, since non-whites remain underrepresented in both undergraduate and graduate degree programs.

Are Women an Underutilized Resource for New Faculty?

There exists, however, one underutilized minority group which offers a potential solution to both problems. Women constitute 50 percent of undergraduate enrollments yet remain broadly underrepresented in tenured faculty positions.

While the status and representation of women in academe has improved since the 1960s resurgence of the women's movement, women faculty remain underrepresented on most campuses. Several recent studies (Justus, Freitag, and Parker 1987; University of Virginia 1988) found that women comprised about one-fourth of the faculty but only about one tenth of the tenured, full professors. Furthermore, the attrition rate among women in academe is higher and women who stay take two to ten years longer for promotion than their male counterparts. Increasing the numbers of female faculty may be the best solution to the predicted teacher shortage; however, we must first address the issues of higher attrition and slower career mobility for women in higher education.

Gender Discrimination: Does It Still Exist?

When gender discrimination exists, it is often subtle and systemic. Academia has long been dominated by men, and the male perspective in policy development, performance evaluation, and interpersonal interactions generally prevails. Student evaluations indicate that women's classroom performance is often evaluated more critically than men's. Research by women or about women is frequently undervalued by male colleagues. Initial salary differentials between men and women increase in favor of men as faculty progress through the ranks. Women take two to ten years longer than men to achieve promotion and tenure; women's greater child care responsibilities may account for some of this differential. Each of these issues leads to a cumulative disadvantage for the female professor. Women who earn doctorates are more likely than men to desire an academic career but are not being hired at equal rates; the cumulative disadvantage also results in women leaving the profession in greater numbers than men.

Are There Differences in Scholarly Productivity Between Men and Women?

There are those who suggest that women are less capable, less competitive, or less productive than men and that these characteristics account for the scarcity of women in higher ranks. While the question of gender difference in scholarly productivity is complex, the evidence suggests that women are as capable and as productive as men in the academic arena. A recent study of highly productive scholars of both sexes (Davis and Astin 1987) found that differences did exist in the type of publication but not in the quality or quantity of work.

Few studies have examined the relationship between marriage and scholarship or parenthood and scholarship. Results of studies which did consider family issues were mixed. In some cases marriage had no effect on women's scholarship, and in other cases it had a positive effect. Parenthood seemed to make scholarly activity more difficult for men and women. No study was found which asked women how they felt about the choices they had made to maintain their scholarly productivity.

How Do Women Manage the Conflicts Between Family and Career?

Nearly one half of the women who stay in academe remain either single or childless, which raises the question of how work/family conflicts influence the choices women make. Women who choose to have children are often pursuing tenure during the peak of their childbearing years. Often, colleagues and universities are not supportive of a woman's choice to be both parent and professor. A faculty career is demanding; the average professor works 55 hours per week. When child care and home responsibilities are added, a woman can work 70 or more hours per week.

Conflicts arising from opposing career and family responsibilities are no longer restricted to women in the workplace. A growing number of men who chose to be highly involved in childrearing are now entering the workforce and are experiencing added stress. Additionally, men in dual career relationships can no longer expect the career and family support offered by traditional wives. Interviews with men and women faculty reveal that both are experiencing stress in balancing careers and families and are finding their universities largely unresponsive.

What Can Universities Do?

The climate of college and university campuses that has prevented women from achieving their full potential must change if higher education is to resolve issues of faculty diversity and the impending shortage of qualified teachers. Formal and informal policies which consider the needs of diverse individuals, including the feminine perspective in expectations for faculty, must be broadly adopted and enforced. The following are suggested steps:

1. Address inequities in hiring, promotion, tenure, and salaries of women faculty.

2. Conduct a family responsiveness evaluation of university policies and practices to determine the level of support available to parents and others in a caregiving role and to eliminate factors which add to work/family conflict.

3. Develop a recruitment and hiring policy which is responsive to dual-career couples. A placement program for faculty spouses is one option.

4. Adopt a maternity policy which takes into account the special role of faculty. It is difficult for a woman professor to leave teaching if childbirth occurs in the middle of the semester. Students need consistency in faculty expectations of work and evaluation. The university should find ways of making alternative assignments during the semester of birth so that students do not have to adjust to a new professor midterm. Additionally, deans and other faculty must be made aware of maternity leave policies and support the woman's right to a leave. Maternity leave must be made viable for women faculty.

5. Adopt a family leave policy and encourage new parents to take advantage of it. Neither mother nor father should

feel pressure not to use the allotted family leave. Allow a minimum of three months and make it paid, if possible. Maintain fringe benefits during the parental leave whether or not it is paid. Make family leave available for the care of a sick child, spouse, or elderly parent. Define *family* broadly to include all family configurations.

6. Allow new parents options to reduce their teaching load or committee assignments for the semester or year following childbirth or adoption. Make similar options available for other types of family leave.

7. Stop the tenure clock for one year for the birth or adoption of each child or for severe family crises. Stopping the tenure clock should not be viewed in a negative manner at the time of tenure review.

8. Study the feasibility of providing on-campus child care. If universities are large enough, they should be able to support a child care facility. Finding adequate child care is a major concern of parents. Leaving a young child some distance from work is stressful.

9. Recognize that employees have a life outside of the university by reducing the number of early morning, late evening, and Saturday obligations.

10. Reexamine the teaching and research expectations for all faculty. Perhaps it is unrealistic to expect faculty to be effective teachers and researchers in light of the changes in the family. Institutions might consider hiring faculty members in either primary research positions or primary teaching positions and evaluate them accordingly.

In academic work there is a high correlation between career and life satisfaction. The university, more than other places of employment, is highly influenced by life outside of work. In addition, universities are training grounds for future leaders and need to offer an effective model on how to balance family and career. Institutions must recognize that children are not only an individual responsibility but are also a social responsibility. Universities which seek creative solutions to the underrepresentation of women in higher education and career/family conflict will also solve the problem of recruiting qualified faculty during a faculty shortage. More importantly, they will be making a significant contribution to the development of a new social order which values the care and nurturing of children and others and the role of caregiver.

ADVISORY BOARD

Alberto Calbrera
Arizona State University

Carol Everly Floyd
Board of Regents of the Regency Universities System
State of Illinois

L. Jackson Newell
University of Utah

Barbara Taylor
Association of Governing Boards of Universities and Colleges

J. Fredericks Volkwein
State University of New York–Albany

Bobby Wright
Pennsylvania State University

CONSULTING EDITORS

Brenda M. Albright
State of Tennessee Higher Education Commission

Walter R. Allen
University of California

William E. Becker
Indiana University

Rose R. Bell
New School for Social Research

Louis W. Bender
Florida State University

Paul T. Brinkman
National Center for Higher Education Management Systems

David G. Brown
University of North Carolina–Asheville

David W. Chapman
State University of New York–Albany

Linda Clement
University of Maryland

Richard A. Couto
Tennessee State University

Peter Frederick
Wabash College

Mildred Garcia
Montclair State College

Edward R. Hines
Illinois State University

Dianne Horgan
Memphis State University

Don Hossler
Indiana University

John L. Howarth
Private Consultant

William Ihlanfeldt
Northwestern University

REVIEW PANEL

Charles Adams
University of Massachusetts–Amherst

Richard Alfred
University of Michigan

Philip G. Altbach
State University of New York at Buffalo

Louis C. Attinasi, Jr.
University of Houston

Ann E. Austin
Vanderbilt University

Robert J. Barak
Iowa State Board of Regents

Alan Bayer
Virginia Polytechnic Institute and State University

John P. Bean
Indiana University

Louis W. Bender
Florida State University

Carol Bland
University of Minnesota

Deane G. Bornheimer
New York University

John A. Centra
Syracuse University

Arthur W. Chickering
George Mason University

Jay L. Chronister
University of Virginia

Mary Jo Clark
San Juan Community College

Shirley M. Clark
Oregon State System of Higher Education

Darrel A. Clowes
Virginia Polytechnic Institute and State University

Robert G. Cope
University of Washington

John W. Creswell
University of Nebraska–Lincoln

Richard Duran
University of California

Larry H. Ebbers
Iowa State University

Kenneth C. Green
University of Southern California

Edward R. Hines
Illinois State University

George D. Kuh
Indiana University–Bloomington

James R. Mingle
State Higher Education Executive Officers

Michael T. Nettles
University of Tennessee

Pedro Reyes
University of Wisconsin–Madison

H. Bradley Sagen
University of Iowa

CONTENTS

FOREWORD

The following facts help to illustrate the current realities of the status of women in higher education faculty:

- Women make up more than 50 percent of the undergraduate enrollment.
- Women make up 25 percent of the entire faculty.
- Women make up only 10 percent of the tenured full professors.
- Women take two to ten years longer for promotion than men.

These dismal statistics indicate that whatever has so far been done to help eliminate gender differences and promote gender equality has not worked. It would seem logical, therefore, that new approaches need to be examined.

The missing link in the logic used to close the gender gap is the acknowledgment that, while men and women are no different intellectually, some major social and family differences continue to affect women's chances of success in the academy. In dual-career families, for example, it is the woman who most often must sacrifice her career for the benefit of the family, and it is the woman who bears more of the responsibility and the resulting distractions of child bearing and rearing. Such differences must be considered in establishing policies for the creation of a more equitable environment.

Nancy Hensel, chair of the Education Department and affirmative action officer at the University of Redlands, brings these differences to light in this report. She shows how changing the current climate on college and university campuses can resolve gender inequalities, solve the impending shortage of faculty, and improve diversity among faculty. Dr. Hensel examines the higher attrition and slower career mobility for women in higher education, gender differences in scholarly productivity, and family/career conflicts for both men and women. She then offers a valuable discussion of the steps progressive universities can take toward true equality.

Gender inequalities are with us. They will not go away until more imaginative methods are used that take into account the realities of life. This report provides a blueprint to help institutions become better grounded and more effective in their approach to resolving gender conflicts.

Jonathan D. Fife
Series Editor, Professor, and
Director, ERIC Clearinghouse on Higher Education

ACKNOWLEDGMENTS

I wish to thank the many persons who helped in the preparation of this manuscript. ERIC provided an initial list of references. Sandy Ritchy and other staff at the University of Redlands library were helpful in gathering materials.

I also would like to thank Christine Maitland, National Education Association, for her encouragement and Anna Mancino and Bud Watson and the anonymous readers for their review of the manuscript and comments. I also appreciate the reflections of the men and women who shared their experiences with work/family conflict. Their identities and characteristics have been changed without altering the essence of their experiences.

Finally, I am grateful for the efforts of my son, James, who helped me in managing my work/family conflict during the preparation of this manuscript.

THE NEED FOR FACULTY IN THE YEAR 2000

American education is facing a severe shortage of qualified teachers at the same time that it is under pressure to diversify its faculties. Colleges and universities must recruit an estimated 335,000 new faculty to meet needs in the next decade, and yet declining enrollments at the nation's graduate institutions suggest those with doctorates will be in short supply. Qualified minorities will be even scarcer, since nonwhites remain underrepresented in both undergraduate and graduate degree programs. There exists, however, one underutilized minority group which offers a potential solution to both problems. Women make up 50 percent of undergraduate enrollments yet remain broadly underrepresented in tenured faculty positions. Increasing the number of female faculty may be the best solution to the predicted teacher shortage; however, we must first identify the reasons for women's underrepresentation in the professorate.

Increasing the number of female faculty may be the best solution to the predicted teacher shortage . . .

The Retiring Professorate

Although warnings about the impending shortage of professors have been making headlines in academic sources for several years (D'Armo 1990; El-Khawas, Marchese, Fryer, and Corrigan 1990; Mooney 1990b), there is still a lack of clarity about exactly how serious the shortage will be. A 1987 study by Lozier and Dooris (Blum 1990d) predicted that there would be a 50 percent increase in the number of faculty retiring by the year 2002. Higher education experienced an unprecedented increase in enrollments in the 1960s when the postwar babies came of age.

In addition to a college-age population increase, parental prosperity and hopes for a better future allowed more young people to obtain a postsecondary education. As a result, colleges and universities hired more faculty within a short time than had ever been previously hired in a comparable period. The massive hiring skewed the age distribution of the faculty, and now, when many of these faculty are nearing retirement, educational institutions are facing higher than normal replacement rates.

While the average college professor is a 47-year-old white male with tenure, about 25 percent of the professorate is 55 years or older and another 34 percent is between 45 and 54 years of age (Russell et al. 1988). These are the professors Lozier and Dooris included in their prediction of a 50 percent increase in retirements by the year 2000.

An end to mandatory retirement

In 1986 federal legislation was passed which eliminated mandatory retirement age for most employees; mandatory retirement for professors ends in 1994. A recent study by the TIAA-CREF retirement system found that 76 percent of its policy-holders will not change their minds about the age at which they would like to retire because of the new legislation. Most reported that they still plan to retire at about age 66, and almost one-third of those responding to the survey said that they would seriously consider early retirement if an attractive package were offered. Whether faculty decide to retire at age 66 or teach for a few years longer will depend on the perceived adequacy of their retirement income, their health, and their satisfaction with their work (Gray n.d.).

Planning ahead. The Consortium on Financing Higher Education (COFHE), based on a study of member institutions, predicted that natural turnover or retirement will be minimal until the year 2000. Private universities, which have a more unequal faculty distribution, may face a retirement peak as early as 1994 (COFHE 1987). The California postsecondary system has begun to plan for an impending faculty shortage. Planning studies indicate that the University of California system will need to hire 10,200 new faculty by 2005; 70 percent to replace retiring professors and 30 percent to accommodate expected growth. San Francisco State University, for example, expects to replace 51 percent of its faculty by 2003 because of retirements (El-Khawas et al. 1990).

In 1990 Lozier and Dooris replicated their earlier study and modified their predictions about faculty retirements. Based on a study of 101 institutions, Lozier and Dooris now believe that faculty retirements will increase by only 25 to 40 percent in the next 10 years (as cited in Blum 1990d).

Bowen and Sosa (1989) completed a comprehensive study of faculty replacement and new doctorates in the arts and sciences. They do not completely agree with the findings of Lozier and Dooris and others. Bowen and Sosa suggest that, while there will be many retirements in the next 25 years, the rate of retirements will be relatively flat. Looking at the 25-year period in 5-year increments, Bowen and Sosa predict that, by 1992, 19.3 percent of the present faculty will be gone.

Currently, United States institutions employ 489,164 faculty; using Bowen's and Sosa's estimates, by 1992 about 93,000 will need to be replaced. Replacement rates during the next four 5-year periods range from a high of 17.1 percent between 1992 and 1997 to a low of 14 percent between 2007 and 2012, or between 83,000 and 68,000 faculty. Bowen and Sosa's analysis includes retirements as well as deaths and people quitting the profession.

An Impending Faculty Shortage

Accuracy in predicting the extent of the hiring crisis may be lacking, but institutions are already reporting the early signs of a faculty shortage. Higher education administrators are reporting trends such as the following:

1. Difficulty in recruiting in "hard to hire" areas such as business and engineering;
2. Increased competition to hire top-ranked faculty;
3. Increased raiding of minority faculty and "star" faculty; and
4. A need to develop more attractive recruitment packages which include assistance for spousal employment (Mooney 1990a).

El-Khawas et al. (1990) suggest that universities will face a financial crunch as they pay higher salaries in an attempt to compete for top scholars in a tight market. Such strategies might also increase dissatisfaction among existing faculty or encourage their flight to other institutions in search of higher salaries. Julius Zelmanowitz, associate vice chancellor at the University of California at Santa Barbara (Mooney 1990a), reports that only 65 percent of the top-ranked applicants accepted offers this year, which is down from 75-80 percent four years ago. Since Santa Barbara is an attractive as well as prestigious institution, it may be assumed that more top candidates are receiving multiple job offers from comparable institutions. The California State University system is able to hire only between 40 and 60 percent of its first choice applicants (Los Angeles Times 1990).

Supply and Demand

Bowen and Sosa (1989) predict that the balance between supply and demand will tip markedly to the demand side between 1997 and 2002 when there will be only four candidates for every five open positions. The supply/demand ratio between 1977 and 1987 was 1.6 applicants to every position. The ratio in arts and sciences will drop to between 0.79 and 0.84 over the next 25 years unless there is an increase in new doctorates.

New Doctorates

A study by the National Science Board, reported on in January 1990, projected a decline of over 1,500 doctorates in natural science and engineering (D'Armo 1990). Three months later, *The Chronicle of Higher Education* reported an increase in applications to doctoral programs of 2-2.5 percent (Blum 1990c). While the number of Ph.D.s awarded over the past 15 years has remained relatively stable, fewer graduates are choosing academic careers. The number of American students receiving Ph.D.s has declined by about 8 percent in the 10-year period between 1978 and 1988, and the number of degrees awarded to minority students has declined by 22 percent in the same period. The stability in doctorate degrees awarded is attributed to an increase in foreign students, most of whom return home after degree completion (Mooney 1990b). In 1987 about one-fourth of all doctorates in the United States (5,600 candidates) were earned by non-U.S. residents, compared with 600 nonresident candidates in 1958 (Bowen and Sosa 1989).

A depressed market

Doctoral recipients faced a depressed academic job market for many years. The influx of new faculty in the 1960s occurred shortly before there was a decline in college-age students. The gradual decline in traditional-age students is not expected to reverse itself until 1994. Stories of people with doctorates in philosophy or history driving taxicabs abound. Indeed, there was a period where it could take a recipient of a new doctorate in certain fields several years to find an academic position. Many simply gave up and changed to other professions.

As potential graduate students became aware of the lack of faculty positions, many either did not begin graduate studies or did not complete their programs. Bowen and Sosa (1989) predict a further decline in the number of U.S. residents pursuing doctoral studies until 1992. In addition to the decline in actual numbers of U.S. resident doctoral students, there is also a trend for new doctorates to seek employment outside of academe. Industry, public schools, government, and other nonacademic sectors are employing larger numbers of doctorates. Bowen and Sosa (1989) report that the percentage of arts and science doctorates employed in universities and colleges declined between 1977 and 1987 in every field except earth sciences.

There is little likelihood that doctoral enrollments will significantly increase unless there are changes in the perceived incentives of an academic career. Militating against attracting new people to the profession are the decline in salaries in actual dollars, the increased cost of graduate study, and the increased length of graduate study.

New Women Doctorates

While doctoral enrollments overall have been declining, the number of women earning doctoral degrees has steadily increased since the beginning of the modern feminist movement. In 1965 there were only 1,759 doctorates awarded to women; however, by 1988 there were 11,790, or an increase from 10.8 percent to 35.8 percent of the total number of doctorates. Since 1973 doctorates awarded to men have decreased (National Research Council 1989). About 10 percent more women than men who receive doctorate degrees plan to seek employment in higher education (Chamberlain 1988). While women seem more interested in professorial careers and their numbers with advanced degrees are increasing, they are not being hired at a proportionate rate. There has been only a slight increase in the labor force participation of women doctorates in higher education (Heath and Tuckman 1989).

Part-time Faculty

Institutions are hiring an increased number of part-time faculty (Maitland 1990), and many of these are women. Nearly 40 percent of the faculty employed at accredited institutions are working as part-time regular, full-time temporary, or part-time temporary faculty (Russell, Cox, and Williamson 1988). Most of the part-time faculty are women. In a majority of fields the growth of female part-time faculty exceeded the growth of female doctorates. Heath and Tuckman attribute this trend to the desire of women to work only on a part-time basis.

Abel (1984) reports that women are more likely than men to be hired in non-career-ladder and part-time positions. Part-time employees receive no fringe benefits, have no job security, and are paid proportionately less than full-time faculty.

Some part-time faculty, more women than men, are expected to participate in department meetings, advise students, and serve on committees. This may be because more women than men rely on part-time faculty positions as their sole employment. Men are more likely to have other full-time positions and, therefore, would not be expected to participate in university life beyond teaching their assigned classes.

Often the investment of otherwise unemployed part-time faculty in the institution is considerable. Women in part-time or non-career-ladder positions are possible recruits to address the coming shortage of faculty. If Heath and Tuckman's assumptions are true about the desirability of part-time employment, institutions must examine what women perceive as the barriers to full-time employment or the incentives needed to encourage full-time employment.

Faculty Diversity

Colleges and universities are under intense pressure to increase the diversity of the faculty. Minority enrollment in undergraduate and graduate education has declined since the height of the civil rights movement. The minority population of the United States, however, is increasing. To stop the further creation of a minority underclass, minority students must pursue postsecondary education.

But adjustment of minority women students to the academic environment can be difficult. Many minority students will be the first generation in their family to attend college. A significant number of capable minority students will arrive on campus underprepared by their home and educational background to meet the challenges of a university education (Rose 1989). Women minority students may be breaking with the traditional gender roles of their family and culture to obtain an education.

How welcome are minorities on campus?

In the last two years the number of racial incidents on campuses has increased. Minority students do not find predominately white campuses particularly welcoming places. Minority faculty can play a strong role in creating more positive campus climates for minority students as well as providing positive examples of minority achievement for all students (Lyons 1990). Women and minority women faculty are especially valuable role models for female minority students who are challenging traditional role expectations.

Minority faculty, when they are few in numbers, can become isolated and experience difficulty in obtaining promotions and tenure. Campuses must hire a critical mass of minority faculty if significant changes on college campuses are to be realized (Washington and Harvey 1989). Minority women, except black women, continue to lag behind minority men in receiving doctorate degrees (National Research Council 1989). Both racism and sexism confront minority women on campus (Graves 1990), which may account for even less representation of minority women than minority men on university faculties (American Council on Education 1988).

Affirmative action on campus
Affirmative action programs were designed to increase the representation of minorities and women. The failure to employ significant numbers of minority faculty is often blamed on a nearly empty pipeline, yet Washington and Harvey (1989) assert that even the few minorities receiving doctorates are not being hired in proportion to their numbers. Women students, who typically are half of the student body, make up only about one-fourth of the faculty on most campuses. Thus, women are not being hired in proportion to their numbers either. The hiring of new faculty is traditionally handled by senior faculty, who are frequently white males. Selection practices for new faculty have not changed very much to reflect the adoption of affirmative action policies, and faculty often subtly resist affirmative hiring (Washington and Harvey 1989).

An Opportunity for Change
By 2012 only about 80,000 of the 489,164 faculty currently employed on college campuses will remain. During this 22-year period, institutions have an opportunity to change the composition of the faculty to reflect the changing roles of women in society and the increase of minorities in our population. Educational programs will benefit from the different perspectives and research questions these individuals will bring to higher education. Students will benefit from a broadening of their views and an exposure to different ways of thinking, and to different ideas and questions.

To take advantage of this window of opportunity, institutions must assess the campus climate in terms of diversity and examine the reasons why certain groups are underrepresented on the faculty. The questions concerning women's underrepresentation are different from those concerning minority underrepresentation, even though there are similarities in their experiences. Women are attending college in equal numbers to men but are not pursuing graduate degrees in equal numbers and those who pursue graduate degrees are not being hired in equal numbers. Answering the question about women's underrepresentation on the faculty can help to address the coming faculty shortage. More importantly, it can improve the campus environment by questioning traditional assumptions and ways of doing business.

GENDER DISCRIMINATION

The myth of equality in higher education is just that, a myth
(Sandler 1981).

Is Sandler's statement merely part of the rhetoric of gender
politics or is she making an evaluation based on facts about
the status of women on American campuses? If we look at
the statistics for student enrollment, we might assume that
parity has been reached. In the last 20 years, there has been
rapid growth in the participation of women in higher education (Chamberlain 1988). The admissions offices of most
colleges and universities strive for a 50/50 balance of women
and men students and usually achieve it within 1 or 2 percentage points.

In graduate education, too, we have seen enormous strides
in the participation of women students. By the mid-1980s,
women were earning nearly 50 percent of the master's
degrees and about 35 percent of the doctoral degrees granted
in the United States (Chamberlain 1988). At the University
of Virginia, for example, in 1986 the student body was 51 percent female at the undergraduate level, 46 percent female at
the graduate level, and 32 percent female in the professional
programs (University of Virginia 1988).

Does Gender Discrimination Exist in Hiring?

The enrollment figures have not translated into university faculty positions for women, however. The sciences, a field traditionally thought of as male dominated, is a good example
of what is happening in the educational pipeline. In 1984,
1,000 more women than men earned biological science
degrees; 93,000 degrees were awarded to men and 94,000
were awarded to women. Men and women were somewhat
close to parity at the master's level, with 22,000 men earning
master's degrees compared to 17,000 women (Koshland
1988).

At the doctoral level in life sciences, women earned about
50 percent of the doctorates but represented only 36 percent
of those newly hired (Vetter and Babco 1987). In chemistry,
however, the numbers are significantly different, with women
earning only 10 percent of the doctorate degrees and that 10
percent translating to only 4 percent of the new hires for that
year (Koshland 1988).

During the 1970s, more women earned doctorates than previously. They held prominent positions in the American His-

tory Association and were hired more frequently as professional historians. They were not as easily hired for full-time faculty positions although one out of every six women was employed as a part-time history professor, compared to one in twenty men (Winkler 1981).

In some broad fields — biosciences, behavioral sciences and humanities — the doctoral completion rate is nearly equal for men and women (Chamberlain 1988). The hiring rate, however, still does not reach parity. In 1985 the unemployment rate for doctorates in all fields was 0.8 percent, but for women, at 1.8 percent, it was more than twice the overall unemployment rate (Vetter and Babco 1987).

Reskin (1980) studied the professional life chances of women chemists who had received doctorates between 1955 and 1961. While Reskin found no difference in the quality of undergraduate training nor in the prestige of doctoral institutions attended, she found that women were more often hired into lower ranks as research associates, lecturers, and instructors while the men were more likely to be hired into tenure track positions. In 1979 the Committee on the Education and Employment of Women in Science and Engineering found that women were less likely to be hired into tenure track positions. Marital status was also a factor; married women were least likely to hold tenure track positions.

Status of Women Faculty

Several universities have recently completed studies of the status of women on their campuses. Nationwide, in 1988, men made up 73 percent and women 27 percent of the faculty (Russell et al. 1988). Ten years earlier women comprised about one-fourth of the total faculty (Young 1978), which means that the proportion of women has increased by only 2 percent. A small annual increase in the proportion of women faculty in doctoral-granting institutions has been observed over a 10-year period. In 1970-71 women represented 14.7 percent of the faculty, and in 1980-81 their proportion had increased to 18.8 percent — an increase of 4 percent at a time when affirmative action hiring was in place (Hyer 1985).

During approximately the same period, the number of doctorate degrees awarded nearly doubled for women while it declined for men (Weis 1985). While women are earning significantly more doctorates in traditionally female-dominated fields, some of the increase in doctorates also has been in traditionally male-dominated fields.

A 24-year employment analysis of women faculty at the University of Minnesota showed little improvement in their presence or status between 1956 and 1980. In fact, at Minnesota institutions, there was a decline in the percentage of women holding higher ranks (Stecklein and Lorenz 1986). At the University of Virginia (1988), women made up 18.5 percent of all full-time faculty in 1979 and 22 percent in 1986. Justus et al. (1987) found that women made up about 27 percent of the assistant professors but only about 10 percent of the full professors in the institutions surveyed.

The Justus study also concluded that women are concentrated in lower level positions, in two- and four-year colleges rather than in major research universities. Although there are more women in four-year colleges even in such institutions, they have not achieved parity. At the University of Redlands, a small comprehensive liberal arts university, women make up only about 25 percent of the total faculty and there are still some departments without a single woman professor. The Coordinating Committee on the Status of Women at Berkeley found that in 1989 only 15 percent of its full-time tenure track faculty were women but over half of the temporary lecturers were women. The University of California, Berkeley, has a permanent faculty of 1,651. Of the 241 women in this group, only 25 are minority women.

Costs of gender discrimination

Gender discrimination exists on American campuses, and it is very costly. It is costly in a personal sense for those women who successfully completed doctoral degrees only to find that they could not secure employment in their chosen field. It is costly to students who cannot avail themselves of the perspectives represented by the women who were not hired. It is costly for the faculty women already hired, because they remain in a minority position, with all the psychological stresses that can be attributed to underrepresentation. Finally, it is costly to institutions who bear the expense of discrimination law suits, which have been estimated to be in the hundreds of millions of dollars (Robbins and Kahn 1985).

Retention, Promotion, and Tenure

At the current rate of increase, it will take women 90 years to achieve equal representation to men on American cam-

At the current rate of increase, it will take women 90 years to achieve equal representation to men on American campuses...

puses, and not until the year 2149 will 50 percent of the full professors be women (Alpert 1989). This is despite the fact that between 1975 and 1987 there was a 78 percent increase in the number of female full professors. While an increase of 78 percent seems large, it is based on a very small number of women faculty. In 1975 only 2 percent of the faculty were women full professors; in 1987 it advanced to 3 percent, while male full professors made up 38 percent of the whole faculty.

The University of Virgina (1988) reported that women represented 18 percent of the total faculty, but only 8 percent were tenured. Justus, Freitag, and Parker (1987) compared the number of women faculty employed by 15 research universities with Berkeley's figures. They found that the percentage of women employed as assistant professors ranged from a high of 35 percent to a low of 17.4 percent. At the full professor level, the range was from 14 percent to 4.3 percent. Since Justus et al. used 1986 Equal Opportunity reporting figures, one could argue that women are being hired into professorships and that, when they are ready to be considered for promotion, their representation at the full professor level will increase.

A review of hiring rates for women faculty between 1972 and 1985 indicates that women are moving toward parity at the assistant professor level. In 1984-85, 37.5 percent of the assistant professors were women.

Is there a revolving door policy?
Comparable advances over time at the full professor level, however, are difficult to determine. Chamberlain (1988) said that higher education operates by the revolving door theory when it comes to hiring women. Women are hired as assistant professors, but they are not making it into the higher ranks. In a comparison of tenure rates for men and women at the University of Maryland, College Park, however, the rates were nearly equal for the classes of 1973 and 1977, and promotion rates were similar to tenure rates (Ochsner, Brown, and Markevich 1985).

What Ochsner et al. also found was that the promotion rate and tenure rates overall were declining. The reason for the overall decline in tenure rates was not known, but they speculate that the decline may contribute to the perception on campus that it is more difficult for women to achieve tenure than men.

At the University of Tennessee, Chattanooga, faculty women were surveyed (Reid 1987) to determine their perceptions of discrimination. One-third of the faculty women felt there was discrimination in promotion decisions, and one-fourth felt there was discrimination in tenure decisions. Since men hold a greater proportion of the positions, when a woman is denied promotion or tenure, that denial is magnified to create the impression that women are more often denied than men. In addition, since numerically women are a small percentage of the faculty, even with equality in tenure and promotion rates, it still will take years to reach parity at the full professor level.

What studies show

A survey of 12 liberal arts colleges in the Great Lakes region found that men were hired in proportionately greater numbers than women over a five-year period and that the number of women who did not return was greater than that for men. While the study suggested that tenure rates were about equal for men and women, if the women faculty left before tenure in greater numbers and male hiring outproportioned female hiring, then there would be a significantly smaller group of women eligible for tenure (Blackburn and Wylie 1985).

At doctorate-granting institutions, Hyer (1985) found a 13 percent increase in the hiring of women assistant professors over a ten-year period, a 5.2 percent increase at the associate level, and a 0.6 percent increase at the full professor level. The lower percentage of increases at the full and associate professor levels can be attributed in part to the slower promotion rates for women faculty (Astin and Bayer 1972; Forrest, Hotelling, and Kuk 1984; Zuckerman 1987).

In history departments, Winkler (1981) reported that, of the new doctorates hired between 1970 and 1974, about one-third of the men had achieved full professorships by 1980, compared to only one-eighth of the women. Matching men and women for years of experience, educational background, and academic discipline, women were still less likely than men to advance in academic rank (Etaugh 1986). Astin and Bayer (1972) found that, even when women obtained their doctorates from prestigious universities and were highly productive, they were still promoted more slowly than men. Women tend to take two to ten years longer than their male colleagues to achieve promotion (Forrest, Hotelling, and Kuk 1984).

In studying promotion rates for assistant professor appointments at Berkeley over a 10-year period, the Coordinating Committee for the Status of Women found little difference in the promotion rate for men and women in the first six years, from 1974 to 1980. In the remaining four years, however, there was a greater difference, with 46 percent of the men being promoted and only 32 percent of the women. Two questions need to be asked:

1. Have women been denied tenure, and as a consequence, left the university, thereby reducing the percentage of promotions?

2. Is there a *glass ceiling* which is preventing women from moving into the higher ranks?

Justus, Freitag, and Parker (1988) believe that women may be dropping out of academia before they reach tenure at a higher rate than men. A study at the University of Wisconsin-Madison (Reed, Douthitt, Ortiz, and Rausch 1988) found that the percentage of women who voluntarily left the university was double that of men. Women were also more likely than men to leave because of negative tenure decisions.

Pursuing tenure
The pursuit of tenure is a stressful journey. Men and women cope with job stress in different ways. These differences may account for women leaving the university at a higher rate than men (Rothblum 1988). Women try to reduce the emotional impact of a stressful situation, but men tend to attack the problem directly. In working toward tenure, women may try to manage the stress by seeking out supportive relationships but may not systematically analyze the requirements for tenure and design a strategy for meeting them. Men, on the other hand, are more likely to take a problem-centered approach and then seek solutions. If the requirements for tenure include three published articles, the male will seek strategies to get three articles published.

Women at Berkeley. The Berkeley report on the status of women found that, on the Berkeley campus, 90 percent of white males, 80 percent of minority males, 67 percent of white women, and 56 percent of minority women were tenured (Coordinating Committee on the Status of Women 1989). Since white males make up about 73 percent of the faculty, it is easy to see that there is a crunch at the top for tenure and that it will be increasingly difficult for women to achieve tenure in institutions which limit the number of tenured positions. Berkeley, an institution where the number of Nobel laureates (11) is more than twice the number of nonwhite female full professors (5), may be a particularly difficult place to achieve promotion and tenure.

Women chemists in the pool studied by Reskin also seem to be having difficulty achieving tenure. In 1970, 80 percent of the men in American institutions were in tenured positions, compared to about 33 percent of the women. Women started out at lower ranks and their early disadvantage tended to stay with them, often throughout their careers.

The "Matthew Effect." A concept developed by Merton, which he called the "Matthew Effect" after the disciple Matthew in the Bible, suggests that those who have received rewards will be given more, while those not initially rewarded will have even more difficulty achieving recognition (1973). This concept appears to be operating in the population studied by Reskin. She found that:

- new women doctorates were more likely to accept one or more postdoctoral appointments than men;

- often these postdoctorate appointments were less prestigious than the ones accepted by men; and

- women took them because tenure track appointments were unavailable to them.

A prestigious postdoctoral appointment can help to secure a tenure track position; thus, the male who starts out ahead is given more advantages. On the other hand, a series of less prestigious postdoctoral appointments can hinder the eventual appointment to a tenure track appointment; thus, those with less will lose even more advantages. Clark and Corcoran (1986) called this same phenomenon "a cumulative disadvantage" and observed that "disproportionately fewer faculty women than men achieve high levels of success in academe" (1986, p. 20). Among recent doctoral groups, the proportion of men achieving tenure exceeded that of women by about 5 to 20 percent, depending on the discipline (Hornig 1980).

Changes at Barnard. Hewlett (1986), an economics professor who was denied tenure at Barnard in the early 1980s, said that between 1973 and 1984 four women assistant professors were turned down for tenure, and within a 13-year period the department changed from being composed of all females to having women make up only 25 percent of its faculty. This is a particularly interesting change since Barnard is a women's college and has an early history of supporting women in careers.

Perhaps the changes at Barnard can be attributed to a shift in faculty loyalties from an institutional to a disciplinary loyalty and an increased specialization within the discipline. Graham (1978) noted that the shift began in the 1920s and that it also included a shift in perception regarding professionalism from personal qualities valuable in teaching to scholarly qualities valuable in publishing. Women spend proportionately more time on the teaching aspects of a faculty career than on research and publication (Chamberlain 1988; Menges and Exum 1983). It may be that, as institutions move toward more disciplinary specialization, women's emphasis on teaching is being devalued and considered not important to a department that may be seeking reputational standing among similar departments.

Women faculty at law schools. In a study of five law schools, Angel (1988) found that about 89 percent of the tenured faculty were men and only 11 percent were women. In these five schools, the number of untenured faculty women was three times greater than the number of tenured faculty women. One might think that this indicates a positive trend, but Angel says that, while 60 percent of the eligible men are tenured, only 31 percent of the eligible women are tenured. When Hofstra Law School opened in 1970, two out of the eight faculty members were women. Between 1970 and 1987, 14 women had passed through the Hofstra Law School faculty; only 5 were granted tenure. By 1987 the percentage of women law professors had declined to only 14 percent; the revolving door policy was apparently in full operation.

Faculty Evaluation

Tenure and promotion rates may be equal at some institutions, but at many institutions women are still having a more difficult time moving up the academic ladder and in some cases even getting a foot on the first rung. If women are leaving universities in greater numbers than men and are not being promoted and tenured at a rate equivalent to men, then institutions must look for the reasons.

Merit, on which promotions and tenure are based, is difficult to determine. Merit is usually judged on teaching ability, publications, and involvement in university governance, and, at research institutions, on the ability to secure external funding. Each area is fraught with difficulty and the opportunity for bias. Publication, for example, is more than mere quantity or even high quality.

A case in point

Recently, a retired UCLA professor was honored for her pioneering research on the mental health of gay men (Shenitz 1990). While her work was instrumental in changing the American Psychological Association's classification of homosexuality as a disease, one can imagine how her work was perceived when first published. Would her work have been judged meritorious by a tenure committee in 1957 before its full impact was known? Academics are expected to conform to an idealized image of the professorate which has been shaped by very traditional male attitudes (Lewis 1975). Research on homosexuality did not fit the norms for scholarship operating in 1957.

Women's academic work is often not taken seriously. Agnes Fay Morgan, chair of the Household Science Department at Berkeley from 1918 to 1954, tried for years to change the name of her department to Nutritional Science. It was not until a man became chair in 1960 that the name was changed because the old name was considered an academic embarrassment (Nerad 1988).

When men evaluate female faculty

Male readers tend to devalue the writing of women in traditionally male-dominated fields unless the writer possesses high status (Isaacs 1981). Females also tend to evaluate women writers more favorably if they believe that the author has high status. The evaluation of male writers, however, is not affected by status (Peck 1978).

Since academic men view scholarship from their male perspective, scholarship from a female perspective can be viewed as 'soft' or less scholarly than their own (Simeone 1987). This can cause problems for women being evaluated for tenure by predominately male peer review committees. Lewis (1975), for example, found that colleague letters of recommendation written for women by men tended to show women as less able and less interesting than men.

No exceptions for Nobel winners. Even women who have won Nobel prizes find that their work does not receive attention equal to that of male Nobel prize winners. Cole (1979) found that women Nobel laureates were lesser known than their male counterparts. Women who make significant contributions to science, he discovered, may actually fare less well than the rank-and-file woman scientist when compared to men of similar status.

Teaching is normally evaluated by students, and there is much controversy over the usefulness of such evaluations. Time of day the class is held, sex of the professor, subject matter, room design, and many other factors contribute to the feelings students have about a particular class. While evaluating faculty effectively is an elusive process, the presence of discrimination has been documented. Much of the evaluation process occurs in secret, and some feel that the secrecy encourages a more open expression of biases (Chamberlain 1988).

Simeone (1987) says that women are seen as a group as less meritorious and that it is a problem of either the woman's nature, performance, or the choices she has made rather than a flaw in the system which might be in need of reevaluation. Hornig (1980) claims that there is much anecdotal evidence to suggest that women are more carefully scrutinized in the review process than men.

An example. A woman serving on a tenure review committee noted that a woman colleague was criticized for a campuswide program she had developed because it was not sufficiently scholarly. The program was designed to address a clearly identified campus need and she was hired specifically to develop it. The program's success was acknowledged, but the scholarly value of it was still questioned. The candidate seemed headed for tenure denial until it was pointed out that she had done exactly what was expected of her and she had done it well.

The woman on the tenure committee thought that the issue would not have been viewed in the same way if the candidate had been male. She also wondered if tenure would have been denied if a woman had not been on the committee (personal communication 1985).

Another example. A black male professor at Claremont Graduate School recently won a discrimination suit because he overheard the tenure committee's deliberations regarding his case. He claimed that his race was brought into the discussion and that it was clear that he was denied tenure not because of lack of qualifications but because his colleagues did not feel comfortable working with a black man (Njeri 1989).

It is doubtful the committee would have been so vocal about their opinions if the deliberations were conducted more openly or if there had been minorities on the committee. The suit cost Claremont $8 million.

Is the tenure system discriminatory?

Many educators have stated that the evaluation system in use in American universities was designed by white men and does not take into consideration the female or minority perspective (Chamberlain 1988; Finkelstein 1984; Simeone 1987). Discrimination in evaluation is more often subtle and indirect than suggested by the Claremont case, but it is fostered because women and minorities are not a significant part of the white male network on most campuses (Menges and Exum 1983).

The low representation of women and minorities deprives them of access to power sources within the university. Because they are more frequently in lower level positions, they do not participate in the higher levels of decision making of the faculty governance structure (Menges and Exum 1983).

Do tenured women promote more women? A critical number of women faculty seem to be needed to develop equity for women. A study of five law schools found that the critical number is 12 percent. An analysis of tenure patterns indicated that, when there are higher proportions of tenured women, untenured women were more likely to achieve tenure. When the number of tenured women was lower, untenured women were more likely to be denied tenure and more likely to leave the university (Chused cited in Angel 1988).

Chused developed an equation to determine the probability that a faculty member would be tenured. He found that the probability for any given faculty member to be tenured was 53.3 percent; for men it was 46.3 percent and for women 7 percent. When the number of tenured women faculty reaches 12 percent, other women faculty are more likely to be granted tenure.

Women's Role on Campus

Other factors may contribute to women's difficulties in moving up the academic ladder. Women teach more hours per week than men (Chamberlain 1988; Hornig 1980; Stecklein and Lorenz 1986) and they seem to value the interaction with students more than men. For this reason, students are more likely to presume upon women professors' time than men's (Grunig 1987).

Women spend an inordinate amount of time advising students outside of class compared to men. Finkelstein (1984) says that women's early socialization may account for their greater interest in teaching and student development. He suggests that universities cannot change the early socialization experiences of women but must adjust employment practices and reward systems to reflect group differences. He then continues:

> It should be recognized, however, that current practices and the current reward system have evolved over time to meet the needs and orientation of the largest number of academics — majority males. It would be reasonable to expect changes to occur only to the extent to which composition of the professorate actually changes, i.e., to the extent that numerically significant minorities emerges that can mobilize significant support for change (p. 242).

His view is particularly interesting since it suggests that those in power need not take any responsibility for change and those on the outside must be the ones to force change. One would hope that universities, as models of enlightened thinking, would take a more proactive view toward social change. Finkelstein may, however, be reflecting a view which is prevalent on many campuses. If so, is it any wonder that women and minorities are underrepresented at higher faculty ranks?

Student Evaluations

Promotion and tenure review committees usually consider student evaluations of teaching as part of the review process. Women typically spend more time teaching and often report that they highly value teaching. If so, women should fare better than men in this aspect of the review. Yet several researchers have studied sex differences in student evaluations and this concept is not necessarily borne out. Ferber and Huber (1975) found that students rated instructors of the opposite sex less favorably and that more students preferred male teachers. They concluded that the sex of the instructor and the sex composition of the class must be considered in student evaluations.

Students would prefer to study with faculty of the same sex.

Other researchers (Elmore and LaPointe 1974, 1975; Wilson and Doyle 1976) found that the instructor's sex was not a significant factor in student evaluations. Kaschak (1978) asked students to evaluate descriptions of faculty in male-dominated, female-dominated, and neutral fields. She found that women students rated male and female faculty equally on effectiveness, concern, likeableness, and excellence but thought female faculty were less powerful than male faculty. Male students, however, tended to rate male faculty higher than female faculty. Students would prefer to study with faculty of the same sex.

Basow and Silberg (1987), Bennett (1982), and Martin (1984) also found sex differences in student evaluations. Women faculty were perceived as having more warmth and personal concern for students. Women faculty, however, received lower ratings on interpersonal contact with students. Access to faculty was not measured, but students seemed to report less satisfaction with the individual contact they had with female professors.

It appears that female professors are judged on the actual contact time, whereas male professors are judged on how accessible they appear to be whether or not the student ever had contact outside of class. Bennett also found that students were less tolerant of female faculty in other areas. They tended to demand a higher level of formal preparation and organization from women. In addition, they were less likely to accept authoritative positions of female professors as balanced viewpoints. Ferber and Huber (1975), however, found that there was little difference in a student's acceptance of the authority of teachers of the opposite sex.

What this research suggests is that, if women are to achieve parity with men in teaching evaluations, they must invest more time in their preparation and time spent with students outside of class. Perhaps this is why women tend to spend more time on teaching than research.

The "Old Boys Network" and Women

Often discrimination on campus is not intentional. It may result simply because an individual has not become a part of the group. In academe, membership in the group is as important as is membership in the peer culture during childhood and adolescence; the consequences of not belonging may be emotionally less harmful but they can be devastating to career progress. Academic success is dependent upon access to pertinent information and the establishment of a supportive interpersonal and social climate which allows opportunities to develop professional skills (Hall and Sandler 1984).

A majority of women (Stokes 1984) believe that they are excluded from the networks on campus. Since, as Finkelstein (1984) suggested, the academic system is designed to reflect a white male majority orientation, women feel outside of the network.

On the outside looking in

Women are excluded from campus networks when they do not participate in decision making, whether it is at the university or department level (Grunig 1987; Hollon and Gemmill 1976). Department decisions are frequently made in "corridor conversations," those brief conversations that occur either outside office doors or in short visits to a professor's office. A tabulation of a male professor's "corridor conversations" found that he held 50 such brief discussions; only 2 were with female colleagues (Kaplan 1985).

Relationships within departments, however, seem to be improving. Women faculty perceive that within their own departments there is a sense of equity based on competence and quality of work. They also feel included in departmental discussions and informal get-togethers (Christianson et al. 1989).

Sometimes decisions, or at least important contacts, are made during social or recreational activities. At one university it became the practice for male faculty to accompany the dean to bowl every Friday afternoon. Women faculty were never invited and, as a result, were probably excluded from discussions of proposals the college was writing or collaboration on research interests (personal communication 1976). In 1990 President Bush appointed someone with no experience in government or ethics law to a top ethics post because he played tennis with the President. Bush was quoted as saying, "I'm a great believer that sports can do wonders for . . . establishing common ground" (Dowd 1990).

When Marina Angel (1988) decided to seek a law school position, she contacted two former law school professors. They suggested only two law schools to which she might apply for a teaching position; one was unaccredited and the other already employed her on a part-time basis. When she asked about attending the American Association of Law Schools recruiting convention, she was told Columbia graduates did not find employment "that way." She was not given any more access to the "old boys" hiring network than the two schools, even though Columbia was a "feeder" school and there were 145 other accredited law schools in the country.

Kaplan (1985) reports that in Australia there is a practice of excluding women from lunch conversations in the faculty club. Men, she reported, tend to sit in all-male groups. If a woman should attempt to join the group, she will find shoulders turned away from her or such rapid conversation that there is little opportunity for her to join in the discussion. While most campuses are not so overt in their rejection of women, female faculty are frequently left out unless there is a conscious effort to be inclusive.

Creating professional networks
The creation of professional networks is a natural process, and one's network tends to consist of people with whom one feels comfortable. Women are likely to have more extensive female networks, and on some campuses they have consciously built female networks and the subsequent power base so that they can have more equal opportunities for col-

laboration, sponsorship, and support.

Caucuses and committees on the status of women have provided a voice for women in professional associations and institutions. These professional subgroups have pressured associations and institutions to provide more representation of women in governance, in conference presentations, and in editorial decision making and to be more responsive to the climate for women (Chamberlain 1988; DeSole and Butler 1990). Some associations, like the American Association of University Professors (AAUP), have encouraged universities to conduct institutional surveys on the status of women (Chamberlain 1988). All of these efforts have focused on the underrepresentation of women in academe and have had some success in addressing the problem.

The Token Woman Professor
When there are only a few women on a campus, they are even more disadvantaged. Tokenism carries with it several inherent problems (Laws 1975; Yoder 1985).

- A lone woman tends to be highly visible and this places additional performance pressures on her. Because of her high visibility she may be singled out for special recognition. When there is a need for a woman to serve on an important committee, the lack of women in a department may mean that a more junior level faculty member is chosen for an assignment that would otherwise be given to senior faculty. Such recognition can cause resentment.

- A token representative presents a contrast with other faculty members, and there may be uncertainty on the part of the dominant members about how to interact with the underrepresented person. This uncertainty can lead to isolation. If it is difficult to know how to interact with someone, then one tends to avoid the interaction.

- The psychological effects of tokenism on the token individual can lead to a decline in self-esteem and eventual withdrawal from further interaction.

Yoder was appointed to a faculty position at a military academy. She was the first civilian faculty hired and was one of only a few women. In addition, she was hired to teach half-time and conduct research half-time; an arrangement that was unique to her. Her tokenism led to serious misunderstandings with her colleagues which she was unable to overcome, and she eventually resigned her position.

Hostility takes a sexual form

Swerdlow (1989) studied women who entered nontraditional blue collar occupations. Some of her findings apply to women entering nontraditional academic careers. She found that women encountered hostility in the workplace which included materials of a sexual nature such as photographs. Women also reported being propositioned by male coworkers and having increased attention paid to their mistakes. A woman seeking admission to a doctoral program at a prestigious research university in the early days of the feminist movement was greeted by the dean with the comment, "Pretty soon we'll be expected to accept dwarfs, too" (personal communication 1976).

How one woman confronted it. Angel (1988) was one of only a few women law professors at Hofstra when she began her career. During the first years of her employment she endured the comments of her male colleagues regarding the physical attributes of female law students. After hearing about "the blond in the front row with the big tits" at the beginning of each semester for several years, she finally confronted the situation. She says:

> By the fourth time, when there was a lull in the conversation, I piped up with, 'Do you know the airline pilot in the second row who drives a Ferrari?' They all agreed they did. I said. 'He looks like he is well hung.' Shocked silence greeted my statement, together with looks that indicated I was insane. However, the comments stopped, at least in my presence (p. 824).

Not all women are as confident as Angel and willing to confront unpleasant situations. Another woman graduate student in a medical department was embarrassed when she discovered that her male colleagues had sexually explicit video games programmed into the department's computer system. When she asked to have them removed there was little understanding about why she found the games offensive. Rather than file a sexual harassment complaint, she left the department (personal communication 1987). Women consciously try to avoid the use of sexist language in professional and social interactions. As the above examples indicate, men are far less likely to do so (Christianson et al. 1989).

How tokenism affects women

Women's ability to work is affected by their representation in a group. Johnson and Schulman (1989) found that women are increasingly disadvantaged as their numbers in a group decrease, while males are advantaged as their numbers decrease. Women's task-activity levels will fall as their numbers in the group decrease, but men's will increase. This would suggest that the lone woman in a department will have a difficult time and that institutions should strive to have more than token representation in each department.

Male/Female Behavior

The white male nature of the work environment places additional cognitive tasks on women. A male assistant professor can look toward his more senior peers and model their behavior. A woman, however, cannot directly model a male's behavior. She must decide if the male behavior would be perceived as appropriate for her and, if not, she must develop an acceptable adaptation (Horgan 1989). If there were senior-level women professors, she could use them as models and her cognitive tasks would be more similar to the male's. McIntosh (1988) described as the "male advantage" the many aspects of everyday work life that males take for granted but that are not part of the female experience.

Different language patterns

When women are few in numbers they also experience interaction difficulties in discussion groups. Tannen (1990) suggests that men and women have different patterns of language and conversation. These patterns often seem to function at cross-purposes. In groups with only one or two women, the woman's conversation is likely to be overlooked because it is not understood. Butler and Geis (1990) found that, in mixed group meetings, there is an implicit assumption that females will defer to males. If a woman should speak out, her action violates the expected pattern of behavior and reflects negatively on her abilities.

The researchers suggest that these are unconscious reactions. Most faculty have what Butler and Geis term "considered" expectations that are egalitarian but their "automatic" expectations are based on traditional stereotypes. In the situation described above, the male colleagues simply may feel that they do not like the woman but not attribute their feelings to her violation of their traditional expectations. Martin (1984) says that the "zone of acceptance" for sex role behavior is more narrowly defined for women than for men. The stereotype of expected behavior for women is deeply ingrained and, according to Heilman, Block, Martell, and Simon (1989), resistant to change.

Differing views of social reality

Gilligan (1982) suggests that men and women perceive social reality in different ways, which leads to different expectations of relationships. These differences can lead to misunderstandings and problems in establishing collegiality. Collegiality is an informal criterion for tenure. Faculty work closely with departmental colleagues and it is natural to seek out those with whom one feels comfortable. People generally feel more at ease working closely with members of the same sex.

For example, a public school administrator was discussing how the central office had changed from a male-dominated to a female-dominated administration. He jokingly suggested that a major change was in the topics of informal conversation, from sports trivia to new brands of make-up. He said that he missed the sports trivia and could not enter into the cosmetic discussions (personal communications 1990). Informal conversations contribute to the sense of camaraderie and belonging in a work environment.

How women's expectations changed

Women had different expectations than men for their careers in the 1970s. Female faculty perceived themselves (Widom and Burke 1978) as lower than males and did not seem to be able to place themselves accurately on a continuum of "well-published" within their department. Perhaps this is because their exclusion from the male network did not provide them with the knowledge of what other department members were writing and publishing. Widom and Burke also found that males' level of desired achievement was toward eminence in their field while this was not as frequently mentioned by women.

In 1989, however, The Carnegie Foundation found that male/female differences in career expectations had largely disappeared. Men and women had similiar interests in teaching and research. Women were only slightly more likely to favor teaching over research and only slightly less involved in work they expected to lead to publication. Clarke (1988) also found few male/female differences in motivation and interest in higher level positions.

Career expectations for men and women may be merging, but the opportunity to succeed is still significantly different for men and women. In extensive interviews with women faculty who had succeeded and those who had not, Aisenberg and Harrington (1988) found that women often did not know the rules of academic life nor understand what was expected of them. Many successful women academics were still struggling with the balance between their professional and personal lives.

Salary Differences

In 1973, women faculty asked the American Association of University Professors to separate salary data for men and women. When AAUP began in 1975 to keep salary statistics based on gender, it found that women were paid less in all categories in all institutions. Since 1975 the organization has found that the salary gap has not narrowed and that it is widening at the assistant professor level (Committee W 1988).

There is no disagreement that women are paid less than men (Barbezat 1988; Bergmann 1985; Noe 1986; Pounder 1989). Even when factors of productivity, experience, academic field, and institution of employment are controlled, men still receive higher salaries than women (Barbezat 1987). The salary difference has actually increased since 1978 (Williams et al. 1987). The salary inequality between men and women is highest at the full professor level. While faculty may come into an institution at a somewhat equal level, the differential increases as they progress up the ladder and women are at an increasing disadvantage (Noe 1986).

Market conditions and salaries

Some institutions hire faculty according to market demand and pay faculty in certain fields higher salaries. Bergmann (1985) suggests that in female-dominated fields the salaries are lower regardless of the market conditions. Staub (1987) thinks that when women move into a field in substantial numbers the salaries become depressed. Gray (1985) does not believe that market factors are the cause of the salary discrepancy. Political science faculty, for example, are paid relatively well and they are mostly male. There is not a shortage in political science nor is there a profession outside of academe that directly employs political science graduates, and yet these factors do not negatively affect political science salaries.

Nursing faculty, on the other hand, are paid less and yet there is a nationwide shortage of nurses and there is a direct employment alternative for nursing faculty. Nursing faculty are mostly women.

Life cycle factors. Johnson and Stafford (1974) attribute some of the salary differential to life cycle factors or the personal choices made by women. About three-fifths of the salary difference can be attributed to the market reaction to women's life choices. In part, they suggest this is true because men and women start out on a relatively equal basis, but the disparity grows during the childbearing and childrearing periods and then narrows toward the end of the career. Johnson and Stafford did not differentiate between married and single women and mothers and childless women. It would be interesting to see what, if any, salary disparities exist when women of different marital and maternal status are compared.

Farber (1977) and Strober and Questor (1977) disagree with the findings of Johnson and Stafford. They suggest that the disparity does not lessen toward the end of the career and that more of the differential can be attributed to sex discrimination than to life cycle demands. Barbezat (1988) found that one-half to two-thirds of the salary differential can be attributed to sex discrimination and is not accounted for by life cycle issues.

What's needed now

More comprehensive research on salary differentiation is needed. More information is needed about the marital and maternal status of the women, whether the woman's career is considered primary in the marriage, and the extent to which the husband/father is involved in childrearing. Answers to these questions would clarify the questions of life cycle issues and sex discrimination in salary discrimination.

Issues of discrimination in salary and retention, promotion, and tenure have resulted in several sex discrimination suits which have been costly to institutions as well as to the individuals involved.

Sex Discrimination in the Courts

Farley (1985) reviewed 250 grievances and found that only a handful of the cases were successful in the courts. LaNoue and Lee (1987) said it is very difficult for plaintiffs to prevail in discrimination suits because judges typically do not like to question the personnel practices of universities.

Another difficulty has been the confidentiality issue. Most promotion and tenure decisions are made by a faculty committee which guards its right to act in a confidential and closed manner. Although a candidate must solicit recommendations from peers, the candidate normally does not have an opportunity to review the documents that make up a promotion or tenure file. The recommendation of the committee is, of course, made known to the candidate, but the actual vote is not. In a case involving the University of Georgia, a professor went to jail rather than reveal how he had voted on a tenure decision.

The Supreme Court steps in

The 1990 Supreme Court decision, *University of Pennsylvania vs. EEOC, 88-493,* should significantly change the way in which universities make promotion and tenure decisions and the ability of plaintiffs to prevail. The decision forces universities to turn confidential committee documents over to the courts when a sex or race discrimination suit has been filed. The American Association of University Professors, as well as many universities, filed briefs on behalf of the University of Pennsylvania.

Some faculty (Blum 1990b; Chronicle of Higher Education 1989; Savage and Gordon 1990) feel that they will not be able to provide honest evaluations if their letters will be open to the candidate. A dean was quoted in the Los Angeles Times (Savage and Gordon 1990) as suggesting that all evaluations will be positive because of the potential for litigation and that the decision would adversely affect the quality of faculty hiring.

The American Federation of Teachers (AFT), however, supports the decision. The AFT is engaged in a suit with the University of California, Berkeley, to open up the files for candidate review. Currently, the university provides summaries of the reviews, but the AFT wants the full text (although names of evaluators can be deleted).

It would seem that the more open system would prevent personal characteristics, sex, or race from being factors in promotion or tenure decisions and force the evaluators to make comments which relate directly to the candidate's ability to perform in the position. Quality of research and publication will always be open to subjective evaluation, however; even here, the evaluator will need to be more specific about why a piece of research or an article is lacking in quality. No longer should work be dismissed simply because it is in a nontraditional field such as women's studies or ethnic studies.

Ramifications in higher education

While plaintiffs have achieved only minimal success in their own cases, the ramifications have been felt throughout higher education. Farley (1985) argues that successful and even some unsuccessful cases have served to sensitize universities to sex discrimination issues and that more doors have been opened for women.

The court found that her scholarship had been downgraded because of her sex.

The Rajender Consent Decree at the Univeristy of Minnesota (Blum 1990c; LaNoue and Lee 1987) may be one such case. Rajender was employed in the chemistry department at the University of Minnesota. She was denied a tenure track appointment, she thought, because of her sex and national origin. In 1973 she filed suit in federal court. In 1980 the university signed a consent decree without admitting fault which paid $1.6 million, agreed to change its recordkeeping system and affirmative action policies and make it easier for women to sue for sex discrimination.

Since the decree, the institution has handled more than 300 cases of sex discrimination at a cost of over $7 million. On campus, some feel that the university would have made the necessary changes without Rajender while others feel that Rajender was responsible for a changed campus climate. While on-campus case results may be mixed, they are not for the plaintiff. Rajender received only $100,000, and the remaining $1.5 million went to pay legal fees. In addition, she said she was no longer able to secure academic employment. She now works as a lawyer for Lawrence Laboratories in Berkeley.

In another case (Blum 1990a), the court made an unusual decision and granted tenure to an English professor who had been turned down for tenure by the provost and president of Boston University after having been approved by department and faculty panels. The court found that her scholarship had been downgraded because of her sex.

Eleanor Swift, a University of California, Berkeley, law school professor, was denied tenure and felt that gender discrimination was the basis. She was able to resolve the tenure dispute in her favor without litigation by negotiating with the university for an anonymous five-person committee mutually agreed upon by herself and the law school dean. Three professors from national law schools and two Berkeley professors from departments outside the law school were appointed to the committee by the Provost of Professional Schools and Colleges.

Given the law school's standards for tenure, Swift's tenure file, and files of six recently tenured men, the committee was asked to determine if the law school's tenure standards applied to her. The panel did not consider the issue of gender discrimination. Swift believes that the comparative evaluation and the anonymous committee used in her case provide a model for a fair and less-costly settlement of tenure disputes (Ashby 1989).

Conclusion

While lawsuits are financially and emotionally draining, they offer women an avenue for protesting sex discrimination. They also open up for full evaluation and disclosure the woman's teaching ability and scholarly productivity. Whether women are as productive as men is a serious question which must be carefully examined.

Gender discrimination is, unfortunately, still an issue on American campuses and must be addressed if women are to be equally represented in higher education.

SCHOLARLY PRODUCTIVITY

Can women's underrepresentation at senior faculty levels and on the faculties of major research universities be attributed to their lack or lesser rate of research and publication productivity?

Several researchers examined the question of gender differences in productivity, and the results furnish mixed answers. Some studies show no differences in the productivity of men and women. Other studies show no differences in quantity of publication or research but show differences in types of publication. Yet other studies found that women are less productive scholars than men. Researchers also examined the relationship between motherhood and research productivity, again with mixed results. Questions regarding productivity are obviously very complex, and there are many variables to consider.

Are Men and Women Scholars Equally Productive?

If given the devilish assignment of transforming budding writers into probable failures, two directives might come to mind: Make them into women. Better yet, make them into women on the faculty of women's colleges (Boice and Kelly 1987, p. 299).

Boice and Kelly begin their discussion of gender differences in scholarly work with that statement which obviously reflects a widely held belief that women have a more difficult time with writing than men. What is surprising, given the opening assumption, is that Boice and Kelly found that men and women publish at about equal rates. They studied men and women faculty at doctoral level universities and at women's colleges and found no significant support for their assumption.

The Boice and Kelly study is not a maverick in the research literature on gender differences in scholarly productivity. Pettibone, Roddy, and Altman (1987) studied school of education faculty to compare gender and rank differences in publishing. They did not find significant differences based on either rank or gender. They found that faculty tended to publish in equal rates regardless of rank or tenure status. The lack of publishing differences between the sexes based on rank or tenure status is important in considering the reasons for the underrepresentation of women in higher ranks. If junior women faculty are publishing at the same rate as junior men faculty, then it must not be scholarship that is keeping women out of higher ranks. Also, if junior women are publishing in equal rates to men, it suggests that women are leaving the university for reasons other than an inability to compete with men in scholarly productivity.

Boice and Kelly studied faculty in a field with a high proportion of women. Education is a female-dominated field. Does this account for the similarity in publishing rates between the men and women faculty studied in these two groups? Are there personality similarities and work style similarities that play a part in the field people choose, and would these similarities militate against the differences in scholarship which Boice and Kelly expected to find?

Gender Differences in Productivity

Hamovitch and Morganstern (1977) found that women published somewhat less than men. They attributed women's lower level of productivity to a less competitive nature stemming from early socialization experiences. Male scientists, at least between 1955 and 1970, outproduced women scientists in the number of published articles according to Reskin (1980). The men's work was cited more frequently than the women's work, but women had more citations per article than men. Does this suggest

1. that the "old boys" network is involved in males citing each other and therefore contributing to each other's reputational standing?

2. that women are putting more effort into fewer articles which are more worthy of attention?

Male physical educators also publish more than female physical educators (Kovar 1985), at least in unrefereed journals. Women in physical education, however, are publishing books and refereed articles at the same rate as men. Does the higher publication rate in unrefereed articles suggest again the presence of the "old boys" network where editors may ask colleagues or former students to write for them? Kovar also found that men tended to receive more support for their writing efforts in terms of reductions in teaching time to conduct research.

Do men and women have conceptual differences?

Hunter (1989) is convinced that women have different ways of approaching and sharing knowledge and that these conceptual differences emerge in different patterns of scholarly productivity. Men are more often viewed as producers of knowledge and women as consumers of knowledge. This idea comes from the higher visibility of men in academic positions of power as well as in the higher number of male writers in academic journals. Hunter argues that women do produce knowledge but they share it in different ways. Women are far more likely to share their ideas through one-to-one communication and through presentations at conferences.

Presenting one's work for public scrutiny through writing requires a level of confidence that may be more particular to men than women (White and Hernandez 1985). Widom and Burke (1978) found that men generally characterized themselves as above average in their self-evaluation of publishing ability while women were not able to evaluate themselves in comparison to colleagues.

Men are more satisfied than women with the research assistance available to them, and men also tend to spend more time on research than women. Men also seem more satisfied with the quality of research facilities available to them and the teaching assistance they received. Part of the difference in these areas may be accounted for by the higher representation of men in the research institutions and the higher representation of women in the two-year colleges (Russell et al. 1988).

Differences in Reputation

Davis and Astin (1987) studied highly productive scholars to determine if there were differences in reputational standing which could be attributed to gender. They defined highly productive scholars as those who had written 21 or more articles over the span of a career or 5 or more articles during a 2-year period. In their sample, Davis and Astin found no differences in reputational standing determined by gender. They did find some differences in types of publications, however. Women, for example, produced fewer books but more chapters in books. Widom and Burke (1978) found that junior women faculty were more likely to edit a book or a journal and less likely than men to write a book or journal article.

Marital Status, Parenthood, and Productivity

Do family responsibilities make it more difficult for women to conduct research and write for publication? Hamovitch and Morganstern (1977) concluded that, since all women publish about 20 percent fewer articles than men, there was not a relationship between childrearing and scholarly productivity. While they found no relationship between parenthood and publication rate, they suggest that areas not measured in their study, such as the psychological conflict between being a professional and being a mother and women's lower level of competitiveness, might account for women's lower publication rate.

Women mentioned family responsibilities frequently in a survey of counselor educator's perceptions of writing for publication (White and Hernandez 1985). Not a single male respondent, however, mentioned family responsibilities in relationship to writing. Reskin (1980) found that marriage acted as a depressant for women's productivity but as a stimulant for men's. Male and female chemists in Reskin's population published less when they had children than their childless colleagues.

Survival techniques

Cole and Zuckerman conducted a retrospective study of women scientists to see how marriage and motherhood might affect publication rates. The publication rates of three groups of scientific scholars were examined: 1920–1959; 1960–69, and 1970–79. When married women with children were compared to childless women, they found no significant difference in publication rates.

What they found, instead, was that women gave up their leisure time in order to write. Several women commented that it was difficult balancing the responsibilities of a family and conducting research and writing. Women who were successful in their research and writing simply gave up everything that did not relate directly to work and home responsibilities.

Cole and Zuckerman also found that some women in their study were not able to manage both a family and an academic career and they dropped out of the profession after giving birth. Widom and Burke (1978) found that marital status was not a factor in scholarly productivity but having children made a significant difference. Many women, apparently, had decided not to have children, since two-thirds of the married women were childless. Only one-third of the men were childless.

Spousal support. Another factor which might have entered into success in publishing was the availability of spousal support. Over 90 percent of the women had working spouses, mostly in professional careers, while only 45 percent of the men had working spouses, often not in professional careers. Hunter and Kuh (1987), in a study of prolific writers, found that the majority had children and, while many spoke of the delicate balancing act between career and family, they seemed to manage both.

Astin and Davis (1985) found that single women had a lower publishing rate than married women but that single women published more books over the span of their career than married women. The interpretation offered by the researchers is that married women had more access to the male-dominated network and that single women had more concentrated time available to focus on long-term projects such as books.

Tillie Olsen (1978), mother and novelist, describes the difficulty of combining parenthood and writing. The tasks are inherently different. Children's need for nurturing and immediate attention mean constant interruptions, while the writer needs large blocks of concentration time. Olsen talked about the high level of motivation required to overcome the daily demands of motherhood. For some women, the tension may be more than they are able to handle. As a result, Olsen says that there are very few successful writers who are also mothers.

Support and Productivity

Hunter and Kuh (1987) interviewed prolific writers to determine what supported their writing. The 18 writers identified several factors that contributed to their success.

- They participated in professional organizations at the national level. Their participation had several advantages. It tied them into a national network of researchers which facilitated support for their research activities, both financially and through the exchange of information.

- They indicated that a mentor had been very helpful in getting their writing career started.

- They all needed and were able to obtain large blocks of time in which to write. Many said that their colleagues would describe them as "workaholics." Each seemed to genuinely enjoy writing and research, and their success motivated them to continue.

Prolific writers had several characteristics in common. Each had a congenial work environment which encouraged their research and writing and a supportive home environment. Several writers mentioned being able to take advantage of fortuitous opportunities as contributing to their success.

Hunter and Kuh noted several gender differences. The women in the study described themselves as "studious" in their early years and indicated that they had won many honors in high school. Fewer men described themselves in a similar way, nor did the men seem to have achieved as much early recognition for their academic abilities. More men had friends who continued on to graduate school, and the men also had larger collegial networks. The women tended to collaborate more frequently with students by almost twice as much as the men.

Being a member of a productive department can be an advantage. Braxton (1983) found that having productive colleagues can stimulate productivity to a modest degree. The reverse can also be true; an unproductive department can repress productivity in a formerly productive faculty member.

Is the Support System Available to Women?

Various researchers have identified factors that contribute to a professor's ability to conduct research and publish. Are these factors equally available to women and men? Hunter and Kuh (1987) discussed the importance of a national network and a supportive work and home environment. Several factors may mitigate against a support system for women. The underrepresentation of women in academia makes it more difficult for them to develop a national network through participation in professional organizations. The difficulty which women have on the political scene, whether it is in local or federal government, mirrors the difficulties women have in being elected to a national board or being appointed to a national committee. When a woman is either a token or in the minority it can be difficult to establish the type of congenial work relationships which allow for either formal or informal collaboration on research projects.

Some researchers (Reskin 1980; Widom and Burke 1978) identified children as a negative factor in research productivity. Women's more active participation in childrearing certainly makes the home environment less conducive to the type of long and isolated work involved in writing. The lack of positive support may be an overwhelming barrier to publication for some women, while others have found ways to surmount the obstacles.

What Questions Need Asking?

The most important question in the issue of women's scholarly productivity has not been asked:

What price do women pay for productivity?

Some researchers (Astin and Davis 1985; Hunter and Kuh 1987) found that women could be productive scholars. Cole and Zuckerman (1987) found that, while women published less than men, married women with children publish as much as single women. These studies, however, did not ask what price the women paid for their productivity. Studies of workload for men and women faculty indicate they work almost the same number of hours per week (53 for men and 50 for women). Studies (Burden and Googins 1987; Hochschild 1989) of the hours spent on home responsibilities, however, indicate that there are significant differences between men and women. Women indicate that they give up their leisure time and that they cut down on the housework to maintain their career productivity.

No one has asked in the productivity studies if the prolific women writers gave up time spent with their children, if they felt they missed significant parts of their children's growing up, and if they would have made the same choices if they had a chance to begin again.

The psychological price paid by successful women scholars is unknown. It is known that the price paid by women is different, and probably greater, than the price paid by men. Women, even those who were as productive as men, reported feeling more pressure than men. Women, more than men, felt that their institutions placed a high emphasis on publishing (Boice and Kelly 1987). Perhaps the women's equal publishing rates were a result of their perceived higher need to publish.

Cole and Zuckerman (1987) were the only researchers who acknowledged that some women had left their field because they found the dual responsibilities of career and family unmanageable. Little is known about the women who were not prolific writers.

- How many women left the profession because they were not able to find enough time to write and therefore felt they would not have been able to achieve promotion and tenure?

- What would these women have contribed if they had stayed in the profession? Would their voices have been worth listening to or doesn't it matter that they left unheard?

- Did the women who left value family more than the women who stayed or did they simply have lower energy levels?

- Would someone who could not successfully balance family and career ask different research questions?

- Should institutions make room for a wider range of commitment to the profession and a wider interpretation of faculty responsibilities?

Conclusion

Many questions remain unanswered, and the available evidence is somewhat inconclusive. Clearly, some women are able to produce research and publications at a rate equivalent to many men. Other women are not. In some cases marriage supports women's efforts at publishing. In most cases the presence of children serves as a deterrent to women's publishing efforts. There are other factors as well. Lack of confidence, lack of knowledge of the system, and a limited collegial network all contribute to a lowered productivity rate for women.

It is in the interest of the institution to increase the job satisfaction as well as the level of performance of all faculty, but especially the underrepresented groups even if it is "a devilish assignment."

WORK/FAMILY CONFLICTS

The call of the feminist movement in the 1960s and 1970s was that women could have it all; they could be mothers, wives, and careerists and enjoy success in each area. But what did it mean to "have it all"? The concept of women working was not new, but the difference in the 1980s was that women began to view their work not just as a means to provide additional support for the family but as a career with demands for commitment equal to that of the family. Women's orientation toward work changed and became more similar to men's view toward work. "Having it all" meant that women found psychological and emotional meaning in work as well as motherhood and marriage.

Identifying the Conflict

What women did not count on, however, was that the demands on their time and emotions would be so much in conflict. Years of observing fathers and husbands actively engaged in careers did not provide examples of the family/career conflict that women were obviously experiencing or of ways to successfully balance career and family responsibilities. Few contemporary women grew up in homes where the mother was as committed to her career as the father was to his career. Female role models were not readily available. The few women who were high achievers in the late 1960s had mothers who were also highly educated and had successful careers (Graham 1978).

Evidence of women's difficulty in resolving the conflict between commitment to family and work can be found in the number of women in top level positions who have families. Few women do.

Studies in the corporate world have found that, while most highly successful men are married and have children, few highly successful women have children and many are not married either. In 1984, the *Wall Street Journal* reported that 52 percent of the women who had achieved the status of vice president or higher were childless, compared to 7 percent of the men. *Fortune* magazine surveyed the 1973 women MBA graduates of Harvard Business School 10 years later and found that 53 percent were childless. Hennig and Jardim (1977) studied 25 women who had reached top management positions in industry and business by 1970. Successful women, they found, paid a high price for their achievements — "until their mid-thirties their personal lives were mortgaged to pay

---

for their careers" (p. xv).

While statistics on women professors with children are not as readily available, at one institution it was found that 17 percent of the female full professors and 82 percent of the male full professors had children (Hensel 1990). Yogev and Vierra (1983) noted a trend at Northwestern University for younger professional women to remain childless because they are not confident that a career and motherhood can be successfully combined. More than two-thirds of the faculty women over 40 had children while less than one-third of the women under 40 had children. Reporting on the status of her study of female doctoral students, Kantrowitz (1981) says that of the 12 women who finished Ph.D. work (1958-63), only 3 hold regular appointments. Of those, only 1 married and had children. The other 9, including Kantrowitz, married and had children but were only able to work part-time and at intervals.

Nearly 100 years ago, Charlotte Perkins Gilman, author, lecturer, and social critic, wrote:

> We have so arranged life that a man may have a house, a family, love, companionship, domesticity and fatherhood and yet remain an active citizen of age and country. We have so arranged life, on the other hand, that a woman must 'choose'; she must either live alone, unloved, uncompanied, uncared for, homeless, childless, with her work in the world for sole consolation; or give up world service for the joys of love, motherhood, and domestic service (1906, p. 496).

While the choices today are not as bleak as those painted by Gilman, women, it seems, still must make a choice between high achievement and having a family; a choice that most men do not have to make.

What women expected

When women began entering the work force in large numbers and competing for high-level careers in the late 1960s, they wanted to be treated equally to men and expected to compete on equal terms. They attended college and graduate school and prepared themselves in other ways for the careers they wanted. What they did not anticipate was that, even with equal educational backgrounds, and equal access guaranteed by law, there were still areas of serious inequality which they could not control. Wendy Williams, testifying at congressional hearings in 1977, said:

> *It is fair to say that most of the disadvantages imposed on women, in the work force and elsewhere, derive from the central reality of the capacity of women to become pregnant and the real and supposed implications of this reality* (United States Congress. Pregnancy Disability Act of 1978, p. 123).

Women did not anticipate the intensity of the conflict between work and family when they began seeking career status equal to that of men.

Time as a Source of Conflict

Time is a critical element in the conflict between work and family. Working women are short of time, and finding enough time to get everything done presents many stressful conflicts. Time is a factor in another way, too. For women who wish to have children, time can be a factor in planning when to have children and assessing the risks of stopping a career to give birth and perhaps to spend a few months or years devoted exclusively to raising a child. Recently, Connie Chung, a popular TV news anchorwoman, announced she would cut back on her career to attempt to have a child. At age 44 she felt she had little time left for childbirth. While her level of success and career demands may be greater than those faced by the typical woman professional, her dilemma is not at all unusual.

When women joined the work force, they did not necessarily give up any other responsibilities. Married women still assume the major responsibility for managing a home, and mothers assume the major responsibility for raising children. Hochschild (1989) found that women work 15 hours per week more than men or, stated another way, they work an extra month of 24-hour days each year. Time is a major area of conflict for professional women. There is never enough time to do the things one must do to advance professionally, to do what needs to be done at home, and to respond to the needs of growing children. Leisure time and sleep are the areas where women borrow time for other responsibilities.

Leisure time and sleep are the areas where women borrow time for other responsibilities.

Equality at home?

Just as it is a myth that women have achieved equality in higher education, so is it a myth that women have achieved equality in the home. In studies of the distribution of housework and child care, researchers (Seeborg 1988) found that men do not share equal responsibility for household and child care duties. Burden and Googins found that, among corporate employees, there was no difference in the amount of housework done by men who had stay-at-home wives and those who had working wives. Interestingly, although many men report that they share equally in housework, when actual hours are tallied or their responses are compared with their wive's responses, the equality is more a perception than a fact.

Seeborg studied 101 couples where at least one partner held a faculty position. She found that men underestimated the time their wives spent on housework and that wives were fairly accurate about the amount of time their husbands spent on housework. It may be that men cannot accurately estimate the amount of time a woman spends doing the laundry, grocery shopping, cooking dinner, or putting the children to bed because they do not regularly perform these activities. If husbands who benefit daily from their wives' household activities are unaware of the amount of time involved in keeping a home going, then it is unlikely that employers, who are mostly male, would be aware of the amount of time women spend working "a second shift" in the evening on home chores.

Parenthood

Deciding when to have a child is a major problem for faculty women. Teaching university level classes is not the sort of work where one can easily find a replacement. Giving birth in the middle of the semester is stressful for the new mother and also is disruptive to her students. Women professors who want to have children often try to "schedule" the birth of their children in the summer when they may not have teaching responsibilities. Scheduling births is not always an easy matter, however.

Women also must think about the time in their career when it is best to have children. One reason Yogev and Vierra may have found younger faculty women remaining childless is that they are postponing childbirth until after they have achieved promotion and tenure. Faculty women often "mortgage" their personal lives to avoid being derailed on the tenure track. The University of Virginia study of the status of women noted that women experienced undue stress because they were striving for tenure during their prime childbearing years.

Tenure may not be the blessing it is perceived to be either. While the woman may safely cut back on research, writing, and university service once she has achieved tenure, she may not feel comfortable in doing so. The awarding of tenure usually means that the professor has achieved a level of recognition among her colleagues. Recognition is often accompanied by more requests to write articles, edit journals, and participate in important university committees, and more access to decision-makers within the university and within one's profession. To give up the opportunities resulting from tenure to have a child is not an easy decision, and women often assess what effect it will have on their career.

Most women have found that there is no ideal time to have a child when one is also involved in a professional career.

The Value of a Woman's Career

In dual-career families, most couples would suggest that both careers are equally valued. Their actions, however, often present contradictory evidence. Which career is more highly valued can be judged in many ways, from simple things like which parent stays home from work to care for a sick child to which spouse is more likely to be the follower when a geographical career change is made.

In a study of dual-career couples in higher education, Weishaar, Chiaravalli, and Jones (1984) found that 75 percent of men interviewed felt their careers were of equal importance to those of their wives; only 15 percent of men thought their own career was more important. The women who were interviewed, however, had a different perception. Just a little over half of women felt that their careers were of equal importance to those of their husbands.

The financial rewards of the career play an understandably large part in the importance attached to a career. Men and women begin their careers at relatively equal levels of pay, but women's wages tend to peak at about age 30 while men's peak at age 45. The birth of the first child creates more role segregation in the family and also has a negative impact on the earning power of the woman (Hood 1983). When a wom-

an's salary is 40 percent or more of her husband's salary or she has a more prestigious job, she is more likely to be viewed as a coprovider. When a woman is perceived as making an equal or nearly equal financial contribution to the family, she is more likely to share power in the marriage. Shared power equates with more involvement of the husband in housework and child care (Gilbert 1985).

From the point of view of family welfare, it is an entirely reasonable expectation that if the man earns more money, he should not have to stay home from work to care for a sick child. Putting the higher paying spouse in jeopardy of losing out on career advancement is not in the best interests of the family. Such decisions, however, place additional burdens on the female employee who must stay home with the sick child.

A woman faculty member found that even when she was the only employed parent, her husband's career still seemed to take precedence over her own. Responding to a university questionnaire on gender differences in retention, she said:

> *The reason is . . . a desperate struggle for time. My husband still has no job and consequently spends more and more time on academic work at home, feeling that he needs to establish himself as a leading scholar in order to find a position. With 3 children under 10, I feel I have a much bigger share of family responsibilities than he does"* (University of Wisconsin 1988, p. 37).

While mobility studies indicate that women are willing to move to secure a better academic appointment, women have constraints on their mobility (Bell 1989; Rosenfeld and Jones 1987). They are likely to take family income and availability of spousal employment into account in decisions to make a geographic move. If the husband's income and career potential are higher than the wife's, then the husband's career is likely to have a higher family priority.

A husband's mobility may have a negative impact on a female professor's career if she has difficulty in finding a new position. Many women find themselves moving from one visiting professorship to another as they follow their husbands without ever establishing a permanent position. Some institutions have recognized the difficulties dual-career couples face in finding two suitable positions. Oregon State University

(Stafford and Spanier 1990) states on all position announce-
ments that it has a policy of being responsive to the needs
of dual-career couples. Oregon provides a placement service
for spouses and collaborates with other local employees.
Other institutions will hire the spouse, if possible, or allow
a couple to share a position when feasible.

Male/Female Differences in Family Orientation

Men's involvement in the family is not usually as intense as
women's. Men report less conflict between work and family
roles (Justus, Freitag, and Parker 1987; Simeone 1987) while
women seem to have a stronger sense of obligation to nurture
the family (Weishaar, Chiaravalli, and Jones 1984). In part,
this difference in orientation toward the family stems from
different social attitudes about maternal and paternal roles
in the family.

A woman rarely is criticized for being too devoted to her
family; she may incur social censure, however, if she appears
overly devoted to her work at her family's expense. She also
does not receive recognition for her devotion to her family.
In the community it is expected that a woman will place a
high priority on family matters and not let work responsibilities interfere with her ability to meet family obligations. At
work she is advised not to mention her family (Berg 1986).

A man, on the other hand, is rarely criticized if he is more
involved with his work than his family. A man who places
work responsibilities ahead of family obligations is viewed
as meeting the expectations of being a good provider. When
the father is working he is making a necessary contribution
to the family, and cannot be criticized for that. If he also is
highly involved with his family, he is praised, since it is not
expected that he should assume many family duties.

That phenomenon is most obvious in the response of society to single parents. A single father is perceived as almost
saintly, while single mothers are perceived as providing
homes that are not quite able to meet the needs of children.

The careers of both men and women can be affected by
family demands. Men in high level management positions
often see the family as interfering with work and report that
they receive their primary satisfaction from work rather than
family activities (Hood 1983). When companies provide parental leave for the birth or adoption of a new child, few men
take advantage of the opportunity (Sheinberg 1988). While

the company may provide parental leave benefits, managers often feel that men are not sufficiently committed to their careers if they take time off for family concerns. Men probably are reluctant to use parental leave because they fear a negative impact on their future career advancement. Women must take some time off from work at the birth of a child, and most would like to take as much time as possible. Women, too, fear the effect of maternity/parental leave on their careers, but many also recognize the importance of caregiving to the young infant and do not want to delegate that responsibility.

Child-rearing: a woman's issue

Child-rearing has long been viewed as a women's issue rather than a social issue. Felice Schwartz, president of Catalyst, recently suggested in the *Harvard Business Review* (1989) that corporations should establish two career tracks for women, one which recognizes that career is a primary interest of women and another which recognizes that family is a primary interest. Women who opt for the career-primary track would be promoted more quickly and would not be restrained by corporate perceptions of family interference in women's abilities to function at levels equal to those of their male colleagues. Women who opt for the family-primary track would be able to take time off for childrearing and essentially would trade opportunities to progress on a fast track to high level management positions for the corporation's indulgence toward family interests.

While severely criticized by feminists, Schwartz recognized that family involvement and work responsibilities often are in serious conflict. Aisenberg and Harrington (1988) suggest that women be given a longer time to achieve tenure and that, when a woman's accomplishments are evaluated at tenure review, her personal responsibilities should be taken into consideration. Polatnick (1984) believes that men do not participate to any significant degree in childrearing because they know that parenthood has an adverse effect on their occupational prospects. Other researchers (Hochschild 1989; Hood 1983) have found that, even in couples who initially plan a marriage based on equal sharing of household and family responsibilities, once the first child arrives roles become more traditional and segregated.

A University of Wisconsin, Madison, study of gender differences in faculty retention found that women spent considerably more time on child care than men, almost two and a half times more (1988). In a question about the availability and quality of child care, 40 percent of the male respondents with children under 10 years of age said the question had no applicability to them. Closer examination of the data found that those responding "not applicable" were married men. Perhaps their wives managed all of the child care arrangements or stayed home to care for the children.

A study of caregiving activities of faculty in a major midwestern university found that nearly 28 percent more men than women reported never having experienced a conflict between the demands of a child and work (Riemenshneider and Harper 1990). Women reported feelings of guilt about work/family conflict almost twice as often as men. Even more disturbing, of the 360 respondents, no man reported delays in tenure or promotion attributed to caregiving responsibilities, but 11 percent of the women experienced delays.

Stress Factors in Academe

Time constraints and role conflicts are significant stressors for women faculty. Ratner (1980) found that employed women average 70 hours of work per week including housework and child care. With the average professor working 55 hours per week, women faculty are likely to work 80 or more hours per week. A University of Wisconsin, Madison, study found that the university was not responsive to the time constraints and role conflicts of women faculty, especially those who were mothers. One woman who was a parent during her probationary period commented:

> As a single mom I found the probationary period the most stressful, unforgiving, lonesome and painful in my life. . . . I did 'make it' but believe it is not a system designed for people without wives — i.e., partners who take care of life while the junior professor gets tenure. I'd say my department (with few exceptions) and the university did nothing to help me as a single mom in a difficult position. Years later it hurts to remember how hard it was (p. 37).

Other women faculty have commented that they feel torn between their need to spend more time at work and more time at home (Witt and Lourick 1988). One journalism professor said that she felt guilty when she was with her children because she should be writing, and when she was writing she felt guilty because she wasn't with her children (McMillan 1987). In the corporate world, employer inflexibility in regard to family issues has an adverse effect on productivity. If an employer is perceived as unsupportive of family concerns, employee stress and job dissatisfaction increase (Rodgers and Rodgers 1989).

Male Work/Family Conflict

Some men have recognized that work/family conflict is not just a woman's issue. These men are fathers who wish to be a significant factor in their children's lives; in doing so, they have given up some of their commitment to work. These fathers' choices and the conflict they feel about their choices are similar to those working mothers face every day. "Attitudes of men concerning work and family issues are rapidly approaching those of women," according to Faith A. Wohl, director of Dupont's Work Force Partnering Division (1989, p. 183).

Family/work conflict for men is also somewhat different from women's conflict. Men's usually higher income places them in the role of the primary provider, and many men see their contributions as providers as a significant indication of their commitment to family (Lacher 1990). Several recent employee surveys have found that many men are feeling conflicts over their desire to be successful in their career as well as successful parents.

In an employee survey conducted by Dupont, almost half of the male workers reported difficulties with child care arrangements. In a similar survey conducted by AT&T, almost three-fourths of the fathers said they were concerned about family issues while at work. Robert Half International, a San Francisco personnel recruiting firm, found in a survey of 1,000 men and women that 74 percent of men would prefer a job that offered more time for family rather than a fast track position. But employers appear unaware of this trend. A survey of 440 Southern California personnel executives found that only 1 in 10 felt that creating family options for employees would increase their competitive advantage in hiring (Schacter 1989).

A survey of women university employees, however, found that women overwhelmingly thought a child care center and parental leave policy would be attractive recruitment strategies (Thorner 1989).

Created in the Male Image

The structure of university professorships reflects the male dominance of not only the university but society at large. Professorships were originally designed for men who had wives at home not only to care for home and children but also to provide support for the man's career. Professors work more hours than nearly every other profession, take the most work home, and in the past were the least likely to spend time with their children or assist their wives with housework (Kanter 1977). This is the legacy inherited by women professors.

While male professors may not have helped their wives in the past, wives provided considerable help to their husbands. A peak into the acknowledgments of books written by professors prior to the 1960s indicates how often authors recognized their wives' "invaluable assistance," which may have included typing, reading and critiquing manuscripts, acting as sounding boards, and sometimes even assisting in the research.

Men received support in other ways as well. The wife was responsible for all domestic matters, including scheduling social affairs which may have helped her husband's career. It has been said that a professorship is really a two-person career. While most men and women can no longer count on their spouse to be available as an unpaid assistant, the university has not changed its expectations of the faculty to reflect two-career families (Miller 1986). Since women are competing with men who assume fewer family responsibilities, the burden for women faculty is especially difficult.

The average faculty workload of 55 hours per week means that many faculty work considerably more hours to achieve promotion and tenure (Yuker 1984). Some institutions, such as the University of Wisconsin, Madison (1988), are beginning to look at these issues, but not enough universities have realized that faculty performance is measured by a structure almost designed for high stress, if not failure.

Changes in the Faculty Career

In the past, a sense of community has been a defining characteristic of universities and colleges. Community came from a set of shared values of reflection, study, search for truth, and critical examination of ideas. Students and professors were mutually engaged in the pursuit of commonly defined intellectual goals. At large universities the sense of community

It has been said that a professorship is really a two-person career.

developed more from engagement in study and research and the acknowledgement that all ideas and hypotheses were open to question than from a deeply personalized approach to education.

At smaller universities the sense of community came from personal engagements as well as common commitment to intellectual pursuits. Professors and their families were involved in students' education. The homes of professors were open to student visits, the wives and children of professors were included in university activities, and the life of the university was the life of the professor and his family. Kanter described this type of career as "absorptive" (1977). This is the extent to which a career draws in the family of the employee and pervades all aspects of the individual's life. The faculty career has been one of high absorption.

Changing times

But times have changed. Bowen and Schuster, as they interviewed faculty across the country, found that the sense of collegiality based on personal relationships had largely disappeared (1986). Collegiality today is based more on common goals than on friendships.

Community. Those who remembered different times lamented the passing of the close university community. Changes outside the university, as well as inside, have made it impossible to maintain the university community as an entity. Faculty may not live in the town or city where the university is located. In some cases, such as UCLA, faculty can no longer afford to buy homes near the university. In other cases, a husband may work on one campus and his wife on another, and the couple will live somewhere in between the two campuses.

Many spouses must choose which activities on which campus will be included in their social lives. They cannot attend all of the expected events for two careers. Inviting students to the professor's home for the last night of class may be too much of a burden when one spouse is not home all day to clean the house and prepare the meal. Faculty may not even live in homes large enough to accommodate a small class of 10 or 12 students. Commuting may make it more difficult for faculty to stay late in the afternoon to talk with students or colleagues. Lunch time may be spent running errands, and so even that social aspect of work may have changed.

Faculty. The nature of the faculty has changed, too. Even though minority and women faculty are still small in proportion to white male faculty, they have had an impact on the community feeling of a campus. It is easier to maintain a sense of community when all members share common beliefs, a common heritage, and a common way of life. This is no longer the case. Many people challenge the traditional curriculum because they think it no longer reflects all elements of the population. They challenge traditional activities because they may be offensive to particular groups of people. And the need to be more respectful of people's differences means that daily interactions between people are challenged.

Language. Language has had to change; some words are no longer in use and other words have been added to our everyday vocabulary. Even the buildings on campus have had to change to accommodate physically handicapped students and faculty. What has not changed is the structure of the university and the expectations of faculty.

Bringing Structures into Line with Reality

The structure of the university must change; at the very least it must change to reflect the realities of the lives of its employees. It would be better if the university could lead the way toward creating a new social order which is healthier and more satisfying for all people involved in the university. Higher education plays a significant role in influencing current social practices and priorities; it also is the training ground for those who will be developing social practices in the future.

Universities must begin to recognize that individuals are more than employees, that they have lives outside of the institution. The contributions that one makes outside of work should be valued as much as those made inside the workplace. The role of a university professor has changed over the years. It has expanded to include research, participation in university governance, and public service as well as teaching. Each area consumes the professor's time, creative energy, and intellect.

Perhaps it is appropriate to examine these roles and determine whether it is still possible to expect faculty to engage in all of them simultaneously.

Teaching

The university's most important mission is to educate the next generation of young people who will become our business, education, political, legal, and medical leaders. To be an effective teacher, one must know the subject thoroughly and know how to present the material in a way which makes it challenging and understandable to students. Effective teachers know how to organize material so that it is engaging to students and stimulates them to pursue the topic beyond what can be discussed in the short timespan of the class.

Research on teaching effectiveness indicates that personal interaction between student and professor is important. Students must feel that professors are approachable and will help them if they experience learning difficulty. Professors must therefore have strong interpersonal skills as well as a knowledge of learning styles and characteristics. As education becomes more inclusive, these tasks become more difficult. Professors are no longer facing only white middle class students with backgrounds similar to their own. Their teaching must respond to student diversity.

The knowledge base in almost every field also has expanded as we move to a more global approach in nearly every discipline. The world is changing rapidly, and changes in one part of the world may affect the organization of a discipline at universities. When the Soviets sent Sputnik into space in 1957, it was not just NASA that felt the impact. The training of scientific researchers in the United States was questioned, as well as the science education of elementary and secondary school teachers. Curricula in these areas were transformed in a relatively short period of time.

Recent events in Eastern Europe also have had an effect on the teaching of history, political science, economics, and sociology on American college campuses. Professors must spend a good deal of time reading and reflecting on these changes as they incorporate them into their classes.

Bowen and Schuster (1986) found that faculty have a sense that they are dealing with infinity, that they will never catch up on all the new knowledge they feel they need in order to teach effectively. The decrease in time for collegial relationships and a decrease in the availability of travel funds has made it more difficult for professors to sort through the growing knowledge base.

When professors' roles expand beyond teaching and teaching itself expands, professors find themselves facing a serious time crunch. There may not be enough time in the day to do all that is expected. One area that may be cut is preparation for teaching. Workload studies seem to indicate that faculty are not working more hours but rather that they are rearranging priorities within the available number of hours (Bowen and Schuster 1986).

Bowen argues that faculty may be suffering from deferred maintenance; they do not have enough time available to adequately maintain their intellectual capital. This, of course, has a direct impact on the quality of teaching they are able to provide.

Research and publication

Research is becoming increasingly important in achieving promotion and tenure. Even on campuses which have been traditionally teaching colleges, research is expected. Younger faculty feel more pressure to publish than has been the case in the past, and this has created a glut of articles for professional journals. Many editors are suggesting that the quality of research and writing which they receive is not very high. Finding the time and funds to do quality research is difficult.

University governance

Traditionally, faculty have participated in university management. At Yeshiva University, faculty participation in university management was so extensive that they were denied the right to bargain collectively because it was determined they were part of management. Faculty serve on search and peer review committees which are responsible for the hiring, firing, and promotion of faculty. They determine university curriculum. They may participate in the budgeting process, in recruiting new students and reviewing admissions policies, and in raising money for the university.

All of these activities take time, and each has become more complex in recent years. Admissions is no longer simply finding students who meet the standards of the institution. Admissions must take into account legal issues of discrimination and immigration, male/female balance, and reaching out to underrepresented groups.

Faculty may grumble about the amount of time spent on committee assignments, but governance on many campuses is a sacred cow and faculty often resist any attempts by the administration to infringe on faculty participation in university governance.

Community service

The community often views faculty as a resource, and the university fosters this attitude as part of its public relations policy. Political science faculty may be asked to advise city government on a new policy, a chemist may be asked to serve on a hazardous waste task force, a psychologist may be asked to assist the public schools in developing a suicide prevention program. These activities also take time, often a great deal of time because they are consultative by nature.

Parental Leave

Establishing maternity and parental leave policies is a step institutions can take to reduce the level of work/family conflict. Few universities have taken even this beginning step, however. Recent surveys of small liberal arts colleges and research universities found that most respondents made few provisions for maternity leave beyond those mandated by the Pregnancy Disability Act (Laughlin and Trout-Baretta 1990; Hensel 1990).

The Pregnancy Disability Act of 1978 (PDA), an amendment to the 1964 Civil Rights Act, included pregnancy-related conditions in the definition of sex discrimination. The PDA requires employers who provide disability leave and disability insurance coverage to consider pregnancy as a covered disability. In addition, employers who guarantee employment upon return from a disability leave must also guarantee employment after a pregnancy leave.

The passage of the PDA was considered a step forward for working women, but it does not solve all of the problems of discrimination related to pregnancy. Since the PDA has been in effect, there has been an increase in the number of lawsuits filed by women who were either fired or passed over for promotion because of pregnancy (Bureau of National Affairs 1987).

In addition, some companies and institutions may use pregnancy as a de facto performance evaluation (Trost 1989). When policies are not carefully spelled out, it is often left to the dean or department head to determine how a leave will be provided. If a faculty member is one the university wants to retain, accommodations might be made and an extended leave may be provided. If, however, the faculty member is one the university does not want to retain, the pregnancy leave may become more difficult.

Policy implications

There is probably little disagreement that a maternity leave of three months or longer would be beneficial for the baby and mother, but there is widespread disagreement about the policy implications. Universities in the process of developing new maternity and/or parental leave policies have wrestled with the questions of equal treatment for men and women or preferential treatment for pregnant women.

In the early days of the feminist movement the demand was for equal treatment, but there is a growing group of feminists who believe that equal treatment is not enough. Some feminists believe that we need a new kind of preferential treatment that recognizes childbirth as a social responsibility (Radigan 1988). In the past, preferential treatment protected women from unpleasant work environments such as evening shift work or certain kinds of physical labor. Protective treatment also limited employment opportunities for women. Few would want to return to this type of protection.

A new approach to preferential treatment of pregnant employees would recognize that equal treatment of men and women does not provide equal access for women. Women who bear children and take primary responsibility for child-rearing are at a disadvantage in the workplace. Preferential treatment in the form of extended maternity leave, promotion practices which take family responsibilities into account, and work schedules that are compatible with family responsibilities would provide more equal access for women.

Only women can bear children and breastfeed their infants. These unique characteristics make them different from men and therefore may warrant special treatment in order to ensure equality. The way in which we define equality for handicapped persons might provide a useful analogy. We take the differences of handicapped individuals into account and make adjustments to ensure equal access. Could the same principle hold true for pregnant women and mothers of young children?

Proponents of equal treatment argue that any provision of special treatment for women may make employers more reluctant to hire and promote women into higher level positions. They also argue that special treatment supports the traditional approach to childrearing and that equal treatment of men and women promotes more shared responsibility for children (Piccirillo 1988). Fathers need the option of parental leave if they are to become more fully involved in raising their young children.

Cost. The cost of providing a comprehensive parental leave program could be quite high. The Chamber of Commerce estimated that full funding of the Family Leave Act would have cost $13 billion (Radigan 1988). Universities facing declining enrollments and increased costs may be reluctant to provide a benefit which is not legally required. The University of Wisconsin (1988), in a survey of similar institutions, found that none of the respondent major research universities provided maternity leave beyond the legal mandate.

In reviewing the number of faculty who gave birth or adopted an infant in a single year, Wisconsin found that only 16 of 311 faculty women became new mothers. The University of Redlands conducted a similar survey of all of its employees over a three-year period and found an average of two pregnancies a year. The number of pregnancies and adoptions is not terribly high. Perhaps it would be less expensive to provide leave than to handle the employee turnover and dissatisfaction resulting from work/family stress.

What experience reveals. Other universities have begun to examine the problems of maternity and professorship. The University of California adopted a systemwide policy of stopping the tenure clock for one year after childbirth. The University of Oregon has recently adopted a similar policy. Such policies recognize that the combined stress of an infant and striving for tenure may be an impossible situation for some women. Women who take advantage of such a policy will find themselves slowed in the tenure and promotion process, but at least they will not be faced with termination if they need more time to meet tenure requirements.

At some universities the tenure clock may be stopped without a specific policy if the woman requests it and her dean approves it. While flexibility is desirable to an extent, the absence of a formal policy places the woman essentially at the mercy of the dean's attitudes toward maternity leave. The University of Minnesota's policy allows for a 12-month unpaid parental leave. New adoptive mothers and fathers may take two weeks of informal leave with pay.

The maintenance of fringe benefits, especially medical insurance, is a critical issue during extended parental leaves. Amherst College, for example, maintains benefit coverage if a woman either works part-time for a semester or takes a semester leave. More often universities require the employee to pay for benefits while on leave. This is especially difficult because the income is reduced and paying for benefits is an added expense.

The health and well-being of the child should be a consideration in the development of parental leave possibilities. If we begin to recognize childrearing as a social responsibility, then universities are likely to be more responsive to this issue. Adrienne Rich (1975) argues that universities have used children in research and in laboratory schools and that now they must begin to pay attention to how children are cared for and socialized. The quality of care provided children is a test of a society's humanism. Rich would like to see universities advocate for more humanistic care for children.

Conclusion

Work/family conflicts, although greater for women, are affecting all employees to some extent. The high level of competition and the expectation that career is of primary importance creates tension in professionals. Universities must begin to look at the way in which a faculty career is structured and carefully examine expectations for promotion and tenure in light of the changes in family configurations and women's roles.

Work/family conflicts will only increase as men are expected by their wives to share more equally in home and child care responsibilities. If universities want to be competitive employers, they must make adjustments in their expectations of faculty.

REAL PEOPLE/REAL PROBLEMS

Women are coping with the difficulties of raising a family and maintaining a successful career. To get a more personal view of how people are coping, research for this monograph included sending 40 questionnaires and in some cases conducting a follow-up telephone interview. Women in the study ranged in age from 27 to 46 at the time of the birth of their first child. All but three were married. They had between one and three children ranging in age from infants to teenagers. The questionnaire was mailed in November 1989. In the 28 returned, most women responded at length, and seemed to want to talk about the topic. In some cases men who also experienced difficulty were identified and were interviewed by telephone.

This section reports the results of the questionnaire and the telephone interviews.

Coping Successfully

Patricia received her doctorate in biology at the age of 26 and had her first child at age 27. She had two children at the time she responded to the questionnaire. She has published 21 articles and has 6 more in preparation. She would be considered a prolific writer by the standards used in the Davis and Astin study. She has also received over $400,000 in grants to support her research and received a postdoctoral fellowship at a research center.

Patricia taught at a prestigious private university for four years and then moved to a large state university. She changed universities because she was offered tenure two years early. The private institution would not grant her tenure until she had completed the obligatory six years. Because she was granted tenure without applying for it, she did not experience the stress associated with the process which many other women describe. Receiving tenure was, however, very important to her because she wanted to have a second child.

She reports that some colleagues were not supportive of her pregnancy. An older childless woman in her department told her that "getting pregnant is a terrible career decision." For her, the most difficult aspects of maintaining a career and caring for a family are the late afternoon meetings and colloquia. "Small children need parents then. I hate that conflict," she says.

She would find her dual responsibilities easier if there were more social acceptance of working and having children. She nursed both babies and feels that good onsite day care would have supported her decision. The message that "professional women should not have children" must be changed, she believes.

Katherine's story. Katherine was 37 when her first child was born. An associate professor of English and a writer, she answered the questions at great length but had no time available to be interviewed by telephone. She took a junior sabbatical during the semester when her child was born and reduced her teaching load by one course the following semester.

When asked about the university's responsiveness to her pregnancy, she said:

The administration is running backwards from this issue. There is no willingness to view maternity leave as something to be guaranteed independent of a sabbatical or summer vacation or semester break — if that's when the baby is born. My baby was born during my junior sabbatical, therefore I considered my six weeks of paid maternity leave absorbed by the sabbatical. The university did not. It is treated as an injury or disability, the timing of which is fated, and compensation, likewise, falls where it falls.

In describing work/family conflict, she said:

I needed more time for work, more time for my child. As an older mother already into the river of my work, I found being at home almost as unbearable as I did beautiful. I didn't get enough sleep to get much work done. When the baby went down for a nap, so did I, involuntarily.

My husband was at work all day; we live far from our parents, so I was 'spelled' by a gifted Hmong woman who came to the house 3 hours a day (with her own three-year-old). . . .

I was conflicted, and felt a failure at mothering, thwarted at writing. The baby pulled at my breast, the typewriter at my brain.

Katherine's husband is an adjunct professor at another college. She felt that parental leave for her husband would have been helpful during the first term after their son's birth. Instead, her husband was asked to take on an additional course when a colleague became ill even though there were many other adjunct professors who would have been happy to teach the course.

She thinks that the religious affiliation of her husband's college leads to a belief that mothers should stay home and take care of babies. Many of her husband's colleagues boast of never having changed a diaper.

Katherine has been fortunate to find a good child care center, but nevertheless she says:

> Onsite day care at my college and my husband's college would be a blessing. At 10 months, my child began going to an infant-toddler center half-time. . . . The center is miles from where we live but at least relatively close to where I work. Fortunately, it is so well run we are thoroughly happy with it. [My son] loves it. . . .
>
> A well-staffed center at our workplace would have been our first preference. A place where at least one of us could put in an appearance daily, have lunch with our little one, play with him outside during the day, talk to the care-providers about him during the day and be there in a flash if anything went wrong.
>
> Those options all exist at the center where he goes, but the convenience does not, so once he is dropped off we do not see him again during the afternoon until it is time to pick him up — unless he is sick, and then it may take them a couple of hours to locate one of us.

Coping with Some Difficulty

Karen, an associate professor of mathematics, has two children, 4 years and 9 months. Her husband is on the faculty of another university. The private university where Karen has taught for eight years does not have an extended maternity leave. It offers disability leave, but Karen did not take it because she could not find a temporary replacement. Her child was born in the mid-semester, and, as she says, "the real difficulty is finding someone to take part of a class and keep grading policy equitable for students." In addition, since she was up for tenure the following semester, she thought she needed the teaching experience. Her husband took an unpaid leave from his position which was not a tenure track position. She was awarded tenure.

Karen describes her colleagues as supportive of childbirth

"I was conflicted, and felt a failure at mothering, thwarted at writing."

and childrearing. She said that her department chair did what he could to ease her situation. In addition, she said she did not feel any particular stigma if she brought her baby to meetings or the office when her child care arrangements failed. She is coming up for promotion to full professor soon and feels she is weak in publication and that may be a barrier to her promotion.

Time is her main barrier. "Teaching and administration loads make enough day-to-day demands that I do not have blocks of time to work on research," she said. "It's also harder to travel to conferences." Karen and a colleague have had a book under way for several years. It is finished but needs editing. Since the birth of her child, she has not had time to focus on the project.

What would have made her pregnancy and the first few months after childbirth easier? Karen said:

Both pregnancies were okay; I didn't mind teaching up to delivery. But I would have liked time after the delivery without immediate deadlines — papers to mark, other business to attend to. The first weeks (with a baby) are very special and I feel I lost much of that specialness.

Beth's story. Beth is a professor of sociology at a large public research university. She and her husband, also a professor, have two children. Beth was hired for her first job in the fall of 1980, became pregnant in November, and had her first child in the summer of 1981 when she was 29 years old. Two years later she had her second child, born in February.

Her university provides three months of maternity leave (covered by the sick leave policy), but she took no leave for either pregnancy. Beth indicated that she felt pressure not to take any leave because it would be viewed as a sign of weakness. She felt that some of her colleagues expected her to fail when she tried to combine both children and a career. She comments, "Although I lived through the experience, my marriage remained intact, and I did receive tenure in 1986, I nearly killed myself." In discussing the conflicts she felt about work and family, Beth states:

I need more time for work. The child demanded what he needed. The work did not demand as loudly. (After my sec-

*ond child was born). . . . the pull of both wanting to be a
mother and successful in my career (was stressful). Students
wanted to discuss their research, I had to administer my
grants, I had to teach my classes, but I had to take care of
the children. If the kids got sick and had to be taken to the
doctor or could not go to day care, I would go over the edge.
Also, I could not work on weekends. The stress was great
on weekends.*

Beth felt that three months off would have helped her cope
with the babies. But, more importantly, she felt that supportive
attitudes on the part of her colleagues would have been the
most help. She felt that her colleagues gave up on her. She
said that their expectation that she would fail served to
encourage her because she developed an attitude of "I'll show
them!" but, nevertheless, it was emotionally stressful.

Paying the Price

Susan was not able to manage childrearing and her first faculty
position. She had a difficult pregnancy and a department
which she did not feel was supportive of combining a scholarly career and motherhood. Susan said:

*The administration was not responsive to the special
demands of childrearing. I think this is the issue more than
pregnancy. The first year of my daughter's life was the fifth
year of my employment at the university. Because I continued to teach as well as care for my child, it was clear that
I would not meet the publication requirements for tenure
that year. So I requested and received permission to delay
application until my sixth year. In his letter requesting this
delay, my department head said that 'the birth of her first
child had a significant, negative effect on the development
of her professional career.'*

*The wording seemed be setting me up for trouble later
on and also revealed a view of childbearing as an illegit-
imate reason for needing additional time to work towards
tenure. The delay in application meant that . . . I would not
have another chance to apply. I was in fact denied tenure
the next year. The Tenure and Promotion Appeals Committee ruled in my favor, but their decision didn't change the
university president's mind. Sex discrimination aggravated*

by my decision to have a child probably was at the core of the denial.

Susan explained that her department head and some others in the department questioned one of her publications because it was in an edited book. She considered their refusal to count the book as discriminatory because the same group granted tenure to a man the previous year who also had one publication in an edited book. "My image as a 'pregnant woman' or 'mother' may have made it even more difficult for these southern 'good old boys' to regard me as a real scholar," she said.

Susan is now teaching at another university which has a heavy teaching load but lower expectations for research and publication. She believes that she will be successful in achieving tenure.

Mary's story. Mary graduated Phi Beta Kappa and summa cum laude from a prestigious private university. After completing a Ph.D. in psychology in 1976, she did postdoctoral work in industrial psychology. Her resume includes 22 published journal articles. She has two children and a supportive husband. Her difficulty stems from trying to accommodate two careers in one family.

Mary said that she and her husband, also a professor, had planned to have a first child while in graduate school. She had three miscarriages and was sick a lot during graduate school as a result. "Faculty there were great," she said, "I think because they already knew and respected me and my work. Also, I wasn't competing with them."

Her first child was born in 1975 and she interviewed for academic jobs that spring. Her husband accompanied her on all interviews to tend the baby between feedings. The couple tried to find jobs together for the next several years. Mary took three temporary jobs hoping they'd become permanent. This, of course, made research difficult and involved many new course preparations plus time moving and hunting for jobs — "all the while caring for an infant."

For a time her husband commuted and was only home on weekends. "Being a single parent and a first year faculty person in a new community was difficult," she said. "I often took my daughter to my office, but I never got the feeling my colleagues (about 25 males and one other female) approved."

When her daughter was a year old, Mary's husband took the year off (unpaid paternity leave) "so I could concentrate on my work," she said. "His colleagues thought he was insane. This definitely was a career setback for him." Mary taught until her second child was born in 1978 and then left teaching for a year.

Then the couple got jobs together, her husband's on a tenure track and hers "temporary and with good prospects." This ushered in two years that were fairly stable. Then her job was terminated. "I decided to throw in the towel and pursue nonacademic jobs," Mary said. She retrained in industrial psychology. The family relocated and she worked in consulting. Though her work involved lots of traveling, by and large she found people in industry more understanding of family needs than people in academia.

In 1985, she joined a psychology department in a tenure line job, "thinking that was what I had hoped for. What I found, instead, was that I was punished for the compromises and the flexibility I had shown over the years." Her punishment took various forms: Because she had not published while working outside of academia, when first year evaluations were given, she was penalized because she had no articles in print — even though she had research started and even submitted. She was given no raise.

Because the department averaged ratings over a three-year period, she carried that "unproductive" year for three years. And since she had changed fields, she was given no credit toward tenure/promotion/salary. She started as a new Ph.D. at a low salary.

By her fourth year, Mary said, she was rated in the top fourth of the department, "but was told I was too far behind to have any hope at tenure." Next she applied for an opening for an associate/full professor in education/psychology at the same institution and was hired. Again, though, she was penalized because of her prior experience which "was too diverse." She was hired at the assistant level, at a lowered salary than was advertised and "so here I am, 41 years old, still an untenured professor."

In assessing her career path, Mary said:

The 'reasons' are more complex than dual family/career responsibilities, but show a typical pattern. Women often have to be flexible to make dual-career and family obliga-

*tions work, but universities devalue flexibility — everyone
has to come out at age 26 or 27, get a job immediately, publish lots from the beginning, all on the same topic. Any gaps
in academic jobs, any changes in research area, and you're
doomed.*

*When academics see my vita, they usually write me off
because I've held too many jobs, taught too many different
courses, done research in too many areas, and done too
many nonacademic things . . . In short, I'm not very employ-
able in academia, despite what I think is a pretty good
record. My vita just doesn't look like a man's.*

*I don't think my situation is much different than many
women's. My husband and I started off equally, with degrees
from the same school. He helped more than any other husband I know. Yet now, he's a full professor, with tenure,
making 50 percent more money. We have two wonderful
kids and an excellent marriage, but I still feel that the system
ought to be able to accommodate me a little better. It's not
that the system doesn't help women; it's that there are significant barriers to anyone who takes a slightly different
career path.*

Mary added that in some ways her husband's success is
another barrier. When he has an appointment with a university
vice president and she has an appointment with a student,
"who cancels to wait for the plumber? When life is a zero sum
game, women lose."

Men Balancing Career and Family

While men do not seem to be having as much difficulty balancing career and family as women, some men have found
the academic system not supportive of their particular
situations.

Bob's story. Bob received his Ph.D. at the age of 25. His first
position was at a private liberal arts institution. He describes
his early years as driven. He wanted to be a good teacher, to
do significant research, and to publish. He was successful in
all areas and was awarded tenure after six years. Then his wife
became pregnant. Initially, he had some reservations about
becoming a parent. When the baby was born, however, he
quickly changed his way of thinking.

His wife was a public school teacher and she returned to work shortly after the baby was born. Bob adjusted his schedule so that he could be home to care for the baby. He said he often found himself saying he could not attend meetings at certain times because he had child care responsibilities. He found that his professional focus was changing. He still enjoyed the contact with students and his teaching, but he was less interested in the research and publishing.

He felt guilty about not maintaining his former work ethos and it bothered him that he was not as available to the university. But he enjoyed his involvement with his daughter and also felt that his life was more balanced. A second child was born two years later. As he became more involved with raising his children, he found that the guilt he felt earlier changed to satisfaction. He was convinced that he was making the right choices, that a healthy balanced life involved commitment to family as well as commitment to work.

While he was able to find support among colleagues for the changes he was making, he felt that the university would not ultimately be flexible enough to value his teaching and commitment to family and allow him to devalue his research. So he resigned his tenured position and moved with his family to another part of the country. Now he is teaching undergraduate students in a research university as a non-tenure track professor. He has taken a significant cut in pay but he has gained the control he wanted over his life. He is able to maintain his own personal sense of integrity by putting his energies into teaching and his family.

While the choices were not easy, Bob describes his life as one of balance and personal satisfaction. He is recognized for his outstanding teaching, he is able to pursue his intellectual interests, and his family is happy. He only wonders why the academic system cannot incorporate such choices into the mainstream. Bob also thinks that universities may be providing role models for students that are perpetuating the conflict between work and family. He remembers an especially bright student who had a great deal of difficulty in deciding what to do after graduation. Her professors were active scholars who encouraged her to pursue a highly competitive career path. Such a path ran counter to some of her personal feelings which were more compatible with the model Bob provided. After much soul searching she found a path that met the various needs she had, but it might have been easier for her if her institution had not presented such a rigid model in the first place.

Gary's story. Gary was well established in his career when his second wife became pregnant. His children from his first marriage lived with their mother except for some time in the summer with him. He had not planned on becoming a father again, but in his mid-forties he was about to do so. It was a first pregnancy for his wife, who was a professional but not in academia. Late in the pregnancy his wife found out she was having twins. The twins were born in the middle of the semester after a difficult birth.

Gary's university did not have an approved parental leave policy, but he asked for some time off anyway. The administration responded that he could not have any leave time since the university did not have a policy. Gary says that he "essentially went on strike." He canceled 13 hours of classes before the administration finally arranged for paid colleague coverage of his classes.

Gary found that his teaching evaluations suffered because of his actions. When he told students what he was doing, about one-third were openly hostile and about one-third were sympathetic. He also thought that his relationship with his colleagues was affected negatively by his actions. Gary is convinced that employers ought to be more responsive to the work/family conflicts of employees.

Jack's story. Jack and his wife became parents when they were in their late thirties. Shortly after the birth they discovered that the infant had serious health problems that required several hospitalizations. Jack did not ask for leave, but resigned some committee assignments. His university was understanding of the situation but he reports that it was difficult to manage his work responsibilities and the stress of his child's illness. Often he spent the night at the hospital and then came to work the next day exhausted.

He and his wife, who also had a professional career, took turns staying with the baby when he was hospitalized or taking care of him when he was home. Jack had not understood the need for parental leave until he found himself confronting the difficulties of a seriously ill child and the demands of his classes and research. He could postpone some research activities, but manuscript deadlines and classes still had to be met.

While his colleagues generally were supportive, he thought the university lacked a formal way to respond. This placed more of a burden on his colleagues to fill in for him.

Steven's story. Steven and his wife decided to adopt children in their mid-forties. As older parents, they were unable to adopt an infant. After waiting two years, they finally adopted two brothers, 6- and 8-years-old. The impact of two children with already defined personalities and some emotional problems was tremendous. Steve and his wife, Anne, found that all of their daily routines were disrupted. In addition, their new sons needed a great deal of attention. If Steve or his wife had to travel for business reasons, they found that the children were afraid they were being left again.

Steve and Anne were both well-established in their careers and were comfortable making decisions to cut back on work-related activities. Steve did not write very much during those first two years, nor did he participate much in committee work and university service.

He is convinced that it would have been an almost impossible challenge if he had been facing the stress of tenure and promotion at the same time that he was solidifying the relationships in his newly formed family. As it was, he experienced much personal stress in temporarily changing the direction of his energies. He found the pull between family and career interests a constant tension.

Often he spent the night at the hospital and then came to work the next day exhausted.

Summary

All the faculty interviewed were concerned about doing well in their career as well as being effective parents. As they described the daily routines of their lives, it became clear that a professorship is an absorbing career. They needed time at home as well as large blocks of time to work on their writing and research. Young children are endlessly demanding, and their demands cannot easily be put off while one finishes one more paragraph or grades one more paper.

The faculty also discovered the limits of their university's commitment to families. Most women indicated that they would have liked a longer leave after childbirth. They wanted some way to temporarily reduce the stress in the chase for tenure, but they did not want to be perceived as uncommitted to their careers. The majority think that the university needs to recognize that faculty have personal lives beyond their careers and that this is important to the well-being of professors.

Universities could be more supportive in reducing work/family conflict by providing extended leave, preferably paid, to faculty in the first year of their children's lives or by allowing reduced teaching loads or committee assignments. Colleagues can also be supportive by not expecting women or men to make a choice between a family and a career.

Some men and women commented that within the university structure it was difficult if one did not fit the mold.

What can be learned from the experiences of these men and women? Family life has changed, but institutions have not kept pace with the changes, and the resultant stress is taking its toll on men and women faculty. The parents interviewed were deeply committed to their career and their children. They did not believe that they should have to choose one over the other; they felt they had a right to be both parent and professional.

The university must find ways of accommodating the needs of professor-parents.

RECOMMENDATIONS

The climate on college and university campuses that has prevented women from achieving their full potential must change if higher education is to resolve issues of faculty diversity and the impending shortage of qualified teachers. Formal policies which consider the needs of diverse individuals, including the feminine perspective in expectations for faculty, must be broadly adopted and enforced.

Listed below are some suggestions on policies to address the most pressing needs of women on college campuses today.

1. Address inequities in hiring, promotion, tenure, and salaries of women faculty.

Women are disadvantaged in academe at entrance and throughout their career. Universities must examine the hiring process to ensure that women are hired into positions for which they are qualified. Once hired, the university must find ways to assure that women have access to mentors, have networks to support scholarship, and are paid equitably compared to men. Proactive strategies are needed to address inequities which might occur as a result of student bias in teaching evaluations or peer bias in research evaluation.

2. Adopt family-responsive hiring practices.

In hiring new faculty, institutions must recognize that many faculty have a life partner who also needs employment. Institutions can develop collaborative arrangements with other local employers in order to locate suitable employment for the faculty spouse/partner. Allowing spouses to share a contract is another means of providing support for dual-career couples.

3. Audit institutional family responsiveness.

Since work/family conflict contributes to women's unequal status, the next step in changing the campus climate is to conduct an institutional audit on family responsiveness. Official policies as well as informal practices must be evaluated to determine the degree of responsiveness to family issues.

Does the university have a specific policy on maternity leave? Many institutions consider sick or disability leave as the umbrella for all leaves of absence. Maternity leave can be planned well in advance; it does not happen suddenly as might an illness or accident. Does the university routinely expect faculty to participate in early morning, late afternoon, or Saturday meetings which might be difficult for parents who must make child care arrangements? Is there an expectation that university activities will extend into the home, such as dinners for students? All of these issues can make a faculty career difficult for parents.

Each campus has a different culture, and administrators need to find out from faculty what aspects of the culture are having a negative impact on family life. In this monograph, family life has been discussed in the context of children, but a responsive university will recognize that not all families include parents and children. Some families include the care of a parent or other relatives, other families may be made up of same sex adults, and other faculty may be single.

The university culture needs to be inclusive of the diversity of family configurations just as it is inclusive of different cultural, racial, and ethnic backgrounds. *The New Agenda of Women for Higher Education* (American Council on Education 1989) calls for institutions to conduct a values inventory which would clarify institutional assumptions and beliefs. The clarification process might serve to affirm the humaneness of the institution or redirect its goals to become a more humane place to work and study.

Maternity policy

Maternity leave is mandated by federal law, but treating maternity leave like any other disability leave is not sufficient for a faculty member. It is difficult to time childbirth to coincide with the academic calendar. If a baby is born in the middle of the semester and the professor takes the six weeks of maternity leave to which she is entitled, it places her students at a disadvantage.

It would be better to offer the pregnant professor alternative assignments to avoid disruption of her classes. She might direct independent studies for one semester or teach an additional class the semester before the baby is born. Perhaps there are nonteaching responsibilities, such as curriculum development, which she might perform for a semester.

Family leave

Universities should explore the possibility of offering family leave, preferably paid leave, for all employees. Most new parents indicate that they need three months to adjust to having a new baby in the home. Three months is also the age when babies usually begin to sleep through the night, allowing the parents to get more rest. Bonding between parent and infant is established in the first three months and then the child is better prepared for nonparental child care.

Maintenance of health insurance is important during family leave, especially if leave is unpaid. Employees sometimes need leave to care for seriously ill children or other ill or elderly family members. Some universities have adopted the term "family leave" in order to make their policies more inclusive. When leave is granted it is important to pay colleagues who assume extra responsibilities. Relying on goodwill or voluntary assistance can cause resentment, which creates stress and additional pressure for the new parent to return to work quickly.

Options for caregivers

Some new parents cannot afford family leave if it is unpaid or they prefer not to take a full leave. They might prefer to continue working if accommodations to their new status are made for a short period of time. Options might include:

- reduced teaching load for one or two semesters;

- scheduling classes at times convenient for child care, usually avoiding the early morning or late afternoon hours;

- scheduling classes on only two or three days per week rather than spread out over the entire week;

- eliminating committee assignments for a semester or year;

- reducing the advising load for a semester;

- providing mechanisms for the faculty member to work at home part of the time, which might include the loan of university equipment to be used at home; and

- providing a parking space close to the office or classroom so the new mother can come and go more easily.

Many of these adjustments are also appropriate when care of a seriously ill child or elderly parent is required.

Stopping the tenure clock

Caring for a new baby and trying to meet the research and writing demands for tenure may be an impossible task for some faculty. Stopping the tenure clock for a year after the birth of a child can reduce the stress for the faculty member and help the institution retain an employee.

Other family concerns also may warrant stopping the tenure clock, but which ones should be written into policy raises difficult questions. Should divorce or serious illness or death of a family member cause the tenure clock to be stopped? Discussion among administrators and faculty can result in humane and fair policies which support the institution's responsiveness to families.

Family leave and childrearing issues

Administrators and faculty must be made aware of the legal mandate for maternity leave and the rationale behind family leave. Having a family leave policy on the books does no good if the campus culture is such that employees do not feel comfortable taking advantage of the benefits to which they are entitled. It is important that both men and women feel they can take leave benefits without negative repercussions.

Corporations have found that parents who are worrying about childrearing concerns are less productive on the job. As a consequence, some corporations are offering parent education classes or discussion groups during the work day. The expertise of psychology, education, or child development faculty could be used to offer classes and discussion groups on caregiving issues for university employees. In addition to the educational benefits of offering such classes, they would also serve as an indicator of the institution's concern for the well-being of families.

Day care issues

Finding quality child care is always difficult, and sometimes it is not available near the place of employment. Parents prefer to have child care nearby so that they can respond quickly if the child becomes ill or is hurt. Large universities may have enough employees with young children that they can offer child care onsite.

Smaller universities or institutions with limited facilities may think about developing a satellite system for child care. In such a system, the institution would identify family day care providers near the university who would provide care. Universities can assist family day care providers in becoming licensed by the appropriate state agency. Assistance might involve paying the licensing fees or providing help in filing the papers.

The university could facilitate a network among providers and offer inservice education on child care and early childhood curriculum. Parents could be referred to day care homes affiliated with the university, but the university would not need to assume responsibility for managing the homes. Institutions might also consider what services can be provided to facilitate the care of sick children or elderly parents.

Conclusion

All of the above recommendations could address immediate problems faced by parents in the first few years of their children's lives. They do not address the fundamental issue of accommodating a faculty career to childrearing, however. The question remains whether faculty are expected to do so many things that they have little time left for the personal aspects of their lives. Is it reasonable to expect that faculty will be excellent teachers, productive researchers and writers, and active participants in university governance and the community outside the university?

The professorate has been called an imperiled national resource (Bowen and Schuster 1986). By not attending to changing social structures and incorporating them into the academic environment we have endangered the professorate. The threat will only get worse as more men and women try to balance the competing demands of a profession and a family. Universities, as institutions which develop analytical skills and new knowledge, must lead the way in establishing a work environment which recognizes the wholeness of an individual. Our children's well-being depends on it — both from the perspective of parents who must nurture their own children and from the perspective of professors who must model humaneness for the next generation.

Time to reexamine expectations

Perhaps it is time to reexamine expectations of faculty and how success is defined for promotion and tenure. Perhaps we need to redefine the faculty role and limit it to either teaching or research. Both men and women have assumed more caregiving responsibilities as a result of the economic need for two incomes in a family and women's desire to fully participate in life outside the home. Recent criticisms of higher education suggest that the pressure to publish has decreased the amount of time faculty devote to teaching. Universities might consider identifying those faculty who wish to engage primarily in teaching and those faculty who wish to engage primarily in research and writing. Expectations for promotion and tenure could reflect the primary emphasis of the professor.

It is often argued that research is what keeps a professor current in the teaching discipline, but this objective could be accomplished in other ways. Departments might have teaching faculty and research faculty. Research faculty could share their findings with teaching faculty and teaching faculty could share their reading and interpretation of literature and the issues of concern in their classes with research faculty.

Institutions would need to carefully orchestrate such a change so that teaching does not take a second place to research. Teachers might also need higher compensation since they may have less access to grants and outside consulting. Such a step, if done well, might improve the sense of a community of scholars by providing faculty more time to discuss the critical issues in their disciplines. It also would improve both teaching and research since faculty would be primarily engaged in what they do best and enjoy most. Most importantly, it could provide men and women faculty the time needed for their caregiving activities.

Education as an advocate for social change

Some people argue that business, institutions, and government would be more humane and nurturing if women were in decision-making positions. It won't happen if women continue to feel that they must fit the male image of a successful professional. Women are beginning to recognize this and are pressuring institutions to change. Men are also recognizing that there are other ways of "doing business" and that institutions must change to allow for the changes which are occurring in family structures. Perhaps the question is not whether institutions would be more humane if women were in control, but rather if institutions were more responsive to human issues, would we develop a generation of young people who can respond in caring ways?

The issue is too important to wait until the critical mass of underrepresented people force the change. In every sector of American life we must take the caring perspective. It is no longer alarmist to suggest that our existence depends upon it.

The educational community must continue to be in the forefront of advocating for social change. We cannot leave such a fundamental concern as resolving the conflict between work and family to work itself out over time. Children growing up in homes where parents have insufficient time to nurture them will become parents who have a limited perspective on the meaning of nurturance. The educational community must put its intellectual and creative resources behind finding answers to this critical problem. If higher education can resolve this conflict, it will become a model for other employ-ers in developing caring employment practices.

The problem is more significant than simply bringing more women into the university. If we can solve the conflict between work and family, everyone will benefit and it is likely that more women will enter and stay in academe. The well-being of the university depends on its ability to recruit and retain a talented professorate. Our national well-being depends on our ability to develop a happy, emotionally healthy, and productive next generation.

REFERENCES

The Educational Resources Information Center (ERIC) Clearinghouse
on Higher Education abstracts and indexes the current literature on
higher education for inclusion in ERIC's data base and announce-
ment in ERIC's monthly bibliographic journal, *Resources in Education* (RIE). Most of these publications are available through the
ERIC Document Reproduction Service (EDRS). For publications cited
in this bibliography that are available from EDRS, ordering number
and price code are included. Readers who wish to order a publication should write to the ERIC Document Reproduction Service,
7420 Fullerton Rd., Suite 110, Springfield VA 22153-2852. (Phone
orders with VISA or MasterCard are taken at 800-443-ERIC or
703-440-1400.) When ordering, please specify the document (ED)
number. Documents are available as noted in microfiche (MF) and
paper copy (PC). If you have the price code ready when you call
EDRS, an exact price can be quoted. The last page of the latest issue
of *Resources in Education* also has the current cost, listed by code.

Abel, E. K. 1984. *Terminal Degrees: The New Job Crisis in Higher Education.* New York: Praeger Publishers.

Aisenberg, N., and Harrington, M. 1988. *Women of Academe: Out-
siders in the Sacred Grove.* Amherst: University of Massachusetts
Press.

Alpert, D. 1989. "Gender Inequity in Academia: An Empirical Analysis." *Initiatives* 52(2): 9–14.

American Council on Education. 1988. *Minorities in Higher Education: Seventh Annual Status Report.* Washington D.C.: American
Council on Education. ED 320 509. 58 pp. MF–01; PC–03.

———. 1989. *The New Agenda of Women for Higher Education:
A Report of the ACE Commission on Women in Higher Education.*
Washington, D.C.: American Council on Education.

Angel, M. 1988. "Women in Legal Education: What It's Like to Be
Part of Perceptual First Wave or the Case of the Disappearing
Woman." *Temple Law Review* 61(3): 799–846.

Ashby, D. 1989. "Questions and Answers." *Berkeley Graduate* 14–
17.

Astin, H. S., and Bayer, A. E. 1972. "Sex Discrimination in Academe."
Educational Record 53(2): 101–18.

Astin, H. S., and Davis, D. 1985. "Research Productivity across the
Life and Career Cycles: Facilitators and Barriers for Women." In
Scholarly Writing and Publishing, edited by M.F. Fox. Boulder,
Colo.: Westview Press.

Barbezat, D. 1987. Salary Differentials or Sex Discrimination? *Population Research and Policy Review* 6(1): 69–84.

———. 1988. "Gender Differences in the Academic Reward System."
In *Academic Labor: Markets and Careers,* edited by D. W. Brene-
man and T. I. K. Youn. New York: Taylor and Franklin.

Basow, S. A., and Silberg, N. T. 1987. "Student Evaluations of College

Professors: Are Female and Male Professors Rated Differently?"
Journal of Educational Psychology 79(1): 308–14.

Bell, R. R. 9 January 1989. "Career Mobility: Does Gender Matter?"
A paper read at the Conference on Women in Higher Education,
San Diego, Calif., January 1989. Mimeographed.

Bennett, S. K. 1982. "Student Perceptions of and Expectations for
Male and Female Instructors: Evidence Relating to Questions of
Gender Bias in Teaching Evaluation." *Journal of Educational Psy-
chology* 74(2): 170–79.

Berg, B. 1986. "The end of the juggler." *Savvy.*

Bergmann, B. R. 1985. " 'Comparable Worth' for Professors." *Academe*
71(4): 8–10.

Blackburn, R. T., and Wylie, N. 1985. "Current Appointment and
Tenure Practice: Their Impact on New Faculty Careers." A paper
presented at the annual meeting of the Association for the Study
of Higher Education, Chicago, March 1985. ED 259 648. 18 pp.
MF–01; PC–01.

Blum, D. E. 3 January 1990a. "Court Tells Boston U. to Tenure a
Woman Ruled Victim of Bias." *Chronicle of Higher Education*
36(16): A13.

———. 17 January 1990b. "Supreme Court Rejects Privacy Claim
for Tenure Files, Says University Must Disclose Information on
Bias Case." *Chronicle of Higher Education* 36(18): 1.

———. 14 March 1990c. "Rise in Applications to Ph.D. Programs
Reported in Universities Across Country." *Chronicle of Higher Education* 36(26): 1+.

———. 4 April 1990d. "More Moderate Increase in Faculty Retirements Predicted in New Study." *Chronicle of Higher Education*
36(29): 16.

———. 23 May 1990e. "Ten Years Later, Questions Abound over Minnesota Sex-Bias Settlement." *Chronicle of Higher Education*
36(39): A13–15.

Boice, R., and Kelly, K. 1987. "Writing Viewed by Disenfranchized
Groups: A Study of Women and Women's College Faculty. *Written
Communications* 4(3): 299–309.

Bowen, H. R., and Schuster, J. H. 1986. *American Pofessors: A National
Resource Imperiled.* New York: Oxford University Press.

Bowen, W. G., and Sosa, J. A. 1989. *Prospects for the Faculty in the
Arts and Sciences: A Study of Factors Affecting Demand and
Supply.* Princeton, N.J.: Princeton University Press.

Braxton, J. M. 1983. "Department Colleagues and Individual Faculty
Publication Productivity." *The Review of Higher Education* 6(2):
112–28.

Burden, D. S., and Googins, B. 1987. *Boston University Balancing
Job and Homelife Study: Managing Work and Family Stress in
Corporations.* Boston: Boston University School of Social Work.

Bureau of National Affairs, Inc. 1987. *Pregnancy and Employment:*

The Complete Handbook on Discrimination, Maternity Leave and Health and Safety. Rockville, Md.: Bureau of National Affairs, Inc.

Butler, D., and Geis, F. L. 1990. "Nonverbal Affect Responses to Male and Female Leaders: Implications for Leadership Evaluations." *Journal of Personality and Social Psychology* 58(1): 48–59.

Carnegie Foundation for the Advancement of Teaching. 1989. *The Condition of the Professorate: Attitudes and Trends.* Princeton, N.J.: The Carnegie Foundation. ED 312 963. 89 pp. MF–01; PC– not available EDRS.

Chamberlain, M. K., ed. 1988. *Women in Academe: Progress and Prospects.* New York: Russell Sage Foundation.

Christianson, M. D.; Macagno-Shange, L.; Staley, K. H.; Stamler, U. L.; and Johnson, M. 1989. "Perceptions of the Work Environment and Implications for Women's Career Choice: A Survey of University Faculty Women." *The Career Development Quarterly* 38: 57–64.

Chronicle of Higher Education. March 29, 1989. "Tenure Rate for Men and Women." 36(28): A17.

Clark, S., and Corcoran, M. 1986. "Perspectives on the Professional Socialization of Women Faculty: A Case of Accumulative Disadvantage?" *Journal of Higher Education* 57(1): 20–43.

Cole, J. R. 1979. *Fair Science: Women in the Scientific Community.* New York: Free Press.

Cole, J. R., and Zuckerman, H. February 1987. "Marriage, Motherhood and Research Performance in Science." *Scientific American* 256: 119–25.

Committee on the Education and Employment of Women in Science and Engineering. 1979. *Climbing the Academic Ladder: Doctoral Women Scientists in Academe.* Washington, D.C.: National Academy of Sciences. ED 180 332. 176 pp. MF–01; PC–08.

Consortium on Financing Higher Education. 1987. *Early Retirement Programs for Faculty: A Survey of Thirty-six Institutions.* Washington, D.C.: Consortium on Financing Higher Education. ED 295 507. 137 pp. MF–01; PC–06.

Coordinating Committee on the Status of Women. March 1989. *Report of the C.C.S.W.* Berkeley: University of California, Berkeley.

D'Armo, J. H. 17 January 1990. "Universities Must Lead the Effort to Avert Impending National Shortage of Ph.D.s." *Chronicle of Higher Education* 36(18): B1+.

Davis, D., and Astin, H. S. 1987. "Reputational Standing in Academe." *Journal of Higher Education* 58(3): 261–75.

DeSole, G., and Butler, M. 1990. "Building an Effective Model for Institutional Change: Women's Committees as Catalyst." *Initiatives* 53(2): 1–l0.

Dowd, M. 6 July 1990. "Aces in the President's Service." *International Herald Tribune.*

El-Khawas, E.; Marchese, T.; Fryer, T. W.; and Corrigan, R. 1990.

"Faculty Shortage: Will our Responses be Adequate?" *Bulletin* 42(10): 3-7.

Elmore, P. B., and LaPointe, K. A. 1974. "Effects of Teacher Sex and Student Sex on the Evaluations of College Instructors." *Journal of Higher Education* 66(3): 386-89.

―――. 1975. "Effect of Teacher Sex, Student Sex, and Teacher Warmth on the Evaluations of College Instructors." *Journal of Higher Educational Psychology* 67(3): 368-74.

Etaugh, C. 1986. "Women Faculty and Administrators in Higher Education: Changes in Their Status Since 1972." *Strategies and Attitudes: Women in Educational Administration,* edited by P. Farrant. Washington D.C.: National Association of Women Deans, Administrators, and Counselors. ED 285 439. 197 pp. MF-01; PC-not available EDRS.

Farber, S. 1977. "The Earnings and Promotion of Women Faculty: Comment." *The American Economic Review* 67(2): 199-206.

Farley, J. 1985. "Women versus Academe: Who's Winning?" *Journal of Social Issues* 41(4): 111-20.

Ferber, M. A., and Huber, J. A. 1975. "Sex of Student and Instructor: A Study of Student Bias." *American Journal of Sociology* 80(4): 949-62.

Finkelstein, M. J. 1984. "The Status of Academic Women: An Assessment of Five Competing Explanations." *The Review of Higher Education* 7(3): 223-46.

Forrest, L.; Hotelling, K.; and Kuk, L. June 1984. *The Elimination of Sexism in University Environments.* Paper presented at the Second Annual Symposium, Student Development through Campus Ecology, Pingree Park, Colo. ED 267 348. 37 pp. MF-01; PC-02.

Fortune. 11 July 1983. "Women at the B-School Today." 108(1): 72.

Gilbert, L. 1985. *Men in Dual Career Families: Current Realities and Future Prospects.* Hillsdale, N.J.: Lawrence Erlbaum Associates.

Gilligan, C. 1982. *In a Different Voice.* Cambridge, Mass.: Harvard University Press.

Gilman C. P. 1906. "The Passing of Matrimony." *Harper's Bazaar,* 495-98.

Graham, P. A. 1978. "Expansion and Exclusion: A History of Women in American Higher Education." *Signs: Journal of Higher Education* 3(4):759-73.

Graves, S. B. 1990. "A Case of Double Jeopardy: Black Women in Higher Education." *Initiatives* 53(1): 3-8.

Gray, K. N. D. *Retirement Plans and Expectations of TIAA-CREF Policy Holders.* New York: TIAA-Cref, External Affair, Policy Holder and Institutional Research.

Gray, M. W. September-October 1985. "The Halls of Ivy and the Halls of Justice: Resisting Sex Discrimination against Faculty Women." *Academe* 71:33-41.

Grunig, L. S. August 1987. "Shattering the 'Glass Ceiling' in Journalism

Education: Sex Discrimination in Promotion and Tenure." Paper presented at the annual meeting of the Association for Education in Journalism and Mass Communications, San Antonio, Tex. ED 281 246. 89 pp.

Hall, R. M., and Sandler, B. 1984. *Out of the Classroom: A Chilly Campus Climate for Women.* Washington, D.C.: Project on the Status and Education of Women, Association of American Colleges. ED 254 125. 22 pp. MF–01; PC–01.

Hamovitch, W., and Morganstern, R. D. 1977. "Children and the Productivity of Academic Women." *Journal of Higher Education* 48(6):633–45.

Heath, J. A., and Tuckman, H. 1989. "The Impact of Labor Markets on the Relative Growth of New Female Doctorates." *Journal of Higher Education* 60(6):704–15.

Heilman, M. E.; Block, D. J.; Martell, R. F.; and Simon, M. C. 1989. "Has Anything Changed? Current Characterization of Men, Women, and Managers." *Journal of Applied Psychology* 74(6):935–42.

Hennig, M., and Jardim, A. 1977. *The Managerial Woman.* Garden City, N.Y.: Anchor Press, Doubleday.

Hensel, N. 1990. "Maternity, Promotion and Tenure: Are They Compatible?" In *Issues for Women in Higher Education,* edited by L. Welsh. New York: Praeger.

Hewlett, S. 1986. *A Lesser Life: The Myth of Women's Liberation in America.* New York: William Morrow and Company, Inc.

Hochschild, A. R. 1975. "Inside the Clockwork of Male Careers." In *Women and the Power to Change,* edited by F. Howe. New York: McGraw-Hill.

———. 1989. *The Second Shift: Working Parents and the Revolution at Home.* New York: Viking.

Hollon, C., and Gemmill, G. R. 1976. "A Comparison of Female and Male Professors on Participation in Decision Making, Job–Related Tension, Job Involvement, and Job Satisfaction." *Education Administration Quarterly* 12(1): 80–93.

Hood, J. C. 1983. *Becoming a Two Job Family.* New York: Praeger.

Horgan, D. D. 1989. "A Cognitive Learning Perspective on Women Becoming Managers." *Journal of Business and Psychology* 3: 299–313.

Hornig, L. S. March 1980. "Untenured and Tenuous: The Status of Women Faculty." *Annals of the American Academy of Political and Social Science* 448: 115–25.

Hunter, D. E. 1989. "Women's Ways of Sharing: Knowledge Dissemination at Professional Conferences." *Initiatives* 52(2): 15–21.

Hunter, D. E., and Kuh, G. D. 1987. "The 'Write Way'." *Journal of Higher Education* 58(4): 443–62.

Hyer, P. B. 1985. "Women Faculty at Doctorate-granting Universities: A Ten-year Progress Report." *Journal of Educational Equity and Leadership* 5(3): 234–49.

Isaacs, M. B. l981. "Sex Role of Stereotyping and the Evaluation of the Performance of Women: Changing Trends." *Psychology of Women Quarterly* 6(2): 187–95.

Johnson, G. E., and Stafford, F. E. 1974. "Earnings and Promotion of Faculty Women." *American Economic Review* 64(6): 888–903.

Johnson, R. A., and Schulman, G. I. 1989. "Gender-role Composition and Role Entrapment in Decision-making Groups." *Gender and Society* 3(3): 355–72.

Justus, J.; Freitag, S. B.; and Parker, L. L. 1987. *The University of California in the Twenty-first Century: Successful Approaches to Faculty Diversity.* Berkeley: University of California.

Kanter, R. B. 1977. *Work and Family in the United States: A Critical Review and Agenda for Research Policy.* New York: Russell Sage Foundation.

Kantrowitz, J. S. l981. "Paying Your Dues Part-time." In *Rocking the Boat: Academic Women and Academic Processes,* edited by G. DeSole and L. Hoffman. New York: Modern Language Association of America.

Kaplan, G. T. 1985. "Coming up with Bright Ideas: Women in Academics." *Vestes* 28(2): 19–22.

Kaschak, E. Spring 1978. "Sex Bias in Student Evaluations of College Professors." *Psychology of Women Quarterly* 2(3): 235–43.

Koshland, D. E. 1988. "Women in Science." *Science* 239(4847): 1473.

Kovar, S. K. 1985. "Woman Faculty Scholarly Productive." Paper presented at conference on women in research, Iowa City, IA. ED 278 327. 13 pp. MF–01; PC–01.

Lacher, I. 1990. 21 October. "Bound for Glory." *The Los Angeles Times* E1+.

Lafontaine, E. 1988. "Eliminating Peer Barriers to Educational Equity for Women." *Initiatives* 51(4): 9–17.

LaNoue, G. R., and Lee, B. A. 1987. *Academics in Court: The Consequences of Faculty Discrimination Legislation.* Ann Arbor: The University of Michigan Press.

Laughlin, P., and Trout-Baretta, M. J. "An Analysis of Maternity, Sick and Family Leave Policies of Sixteen Major Research Universities." Paper presented at International Conference for Women in Higher Education, El Paso, Tex.

Laws, J. L. 1975. "The Psychology of Tokenism: An Analysis." *Sex Roles* 1(1): 51–67.

Lewis, L. S. 1975. *Scaling the Ivory Tower: Merit and Its Limits in Academic Careers.* Baltimore: Johns Hopkins University Press.

Los Angeles Times. 28 January 1990. "Press to Replace Retiring Faculty Forces Changes." Inland Empire section, p. 1.

Lyons, N. 1990. "Once You're in, You Gotta Hold Your Own." *Black Issues in Higher Education* 6(22): 13–14.

McIntosh, M. M. 1988. *White Privilege and Male Privilege: A Personal Account of Coming to See Correspondences through Work in Wom-*

en's Studies. Wellesley, Mass.: Working paper, Wellesley College. Center for Research on Women. Mimeographed. 19 pp.

McKaughan, M., and Kagan, J. February 1986. "The Motherhood Plunge." *Working Woman* 69–73+.

McMillan, L. 4 February 1987. "Job–Related Tension and Anxiety Taking a Toll among Employees in Academe's Stress Factories." *Chronicle of Higher Education* 31(21): 1+

Magid, R. Y. 1983. *Child Care Initiatives for Working Parents: Why Employers Get Involved.* New York: American Management Association.

Maitland, C. 1990. "The Inequitable Treatment of Women in Higher Education." In *Issues for Women in Higher Education,* edited by L. Welsh. New York: Praeger.

Martin, M. 1984. "Power and Authority in the Classroom: Sexist Stereotypes in Teaching Evaluations." *Signs: Journal of Women in Culture and Society* 9(3): 482–92.

Menges, R. J., and Exum, W. H. 1983. "Barriers to Progress of Women and Minority Faculty." *Journal of Higher Education* 54(2): 123–44.

Merton, R. K. 1973. *The Sociology of Science: Theoretical and Empirical Investigations.* Chicago: The University of Chicago Press.

Miller, J. D. 1986. "Family and Work." *Labor Law Journal* 37:484–86.

Mooney, C. A. 24 January 1990a. "Academics Are Divided over High Court Ruling on Tenure Documents." *Chronicle of Higher Education* 36(19): 1+.

———. 18 April 1990b. "Faculty Job Market Slowly Improving, Evidence Indicates." *Chronicle of Higher Education* 36(31): 1+.

———. 26 April 1990c. "Universities Awarded Record Number of Doctorates Last Year: Foreign Students Thought to Account for Much of the Increase." *Chronicle of Higher Education* 36(32): 1+.

National Research Council. 1989. *Summary Report 1988: Doctorate Recipients from United States Universities.* Washington, D.C.: National Academy Press.

Nerad, M. 1988. "The Vicious Cycle of Gender and Status at the University of California, Berkeley, 1918-1954." Paper presented at the annual meeting of the Association for the Study of Higher Education, St. Louis, Mo. ED 803 070. 45 pp. MF–01; PC–02.

Njeri, I. 20 September 1989. "Academia Acrimony: Minority Professors Claim Racism Plays Role in Obtaining Tenure." *Los Angeles Times.* 1: 1.

Noe, N. N. June 1986. "Measures of Salary Inequality." A paper presented at the annual forum of the Association for Institutional Research, Orlando, Fla. ED 280 424. 22 pp. MF–01; PC–01.

Ochsner, N. L.; Brown, M. K.; and Markevich, T. S. 1985. "A Study of Male and Female Faculty Promotion and Tenure Rates." A paper presented at the annual forum of the Association for Institutional

Research, Portland, Oreg. ED 259 685. 27 pp. MF-01; PC-01.

Olsen, T. 1978. *Silences.* New York: Delacorte Press.

Peck, T. 1978. "When Women Evaluate Women, Nothing Succeeds Like Success: The Differential Effects of Status upon Evaluation of Male and Female Professional Adults." *Sex Roles* 4(2): 205-13.

Pettibone, T. J.; Roddy M. E.; and Altman, L. 1987. "Employment Status and Gender in Research Productivity." A paper presented at the annual meeting of the Mid-south Educational Research Association, Mobile, Ala. ED 290 375. 11 pp. MF-01; PC-01.

Piccirillo, M. 1988. "The Legal Background of Parental Leave Policy and Its Implications." In *The Parental Leave Crisis: Toward a National Policy,* edited by E. Zigler and M. Frank. New Haven, Conn.: Yale University Press.

Polatnick, M. R. 1984. "Why Men Don't Rear Children: A Power Analysis." In *Mothering: Essays in Feminist Theory,* edited by Joyce Trebilcot. Totawa, N.J.: Rocoman & Allanheld, Publishers.

Pounder, D. G. 1989. "The Gender Gap in Salaries of Educational Administration Professors." *Education Administration Quarterly* 25(2): 181-201.

Radford, M. F. 1987. *Parental Leave: Judicial and Legislative Trends: Current Practices in the Workplace.* Brookfield, Wis.: International Foundation of Employee Benefit Plans.

Radigan. A. L. 1988. *Concept and Compromise: The Evaluation of Family Leave Legislation in the Congress.* Washington, D.C.: Women's Research and Education Institute.

Ratner, R. S. 1980. *Equal Employment Policy for Women.* Philadelphia: University Press.

Reed, L.; Douthitt, R.; Ortiz B.; and Rausch, D. 1988. "Gender Differences in Faculty Retention at the University of Wisconsin—Madison." Mimeographed. Madison: University of Wisconsin.

Reid, P. T. 1987. "Perceptions of Sex Discrimination Among Female University Faculty and Staff." *Psychology of Women Quarterly* 11(1): 123-28.

Reskin, B. F. 1980. *Sex Differences in the Professional Life Chances of Chemists.* New York: Arno Press.

Riemenschnieder, A., and Harper, K. U. 1990. "Women in Academia: Guilty or Not Guilty? Conflict Between Care Giving and Employment." *Initiatives* 53(2): 27-35.

Rich, A. 1975. "Toward a Woman-centered University." In *Women and the Power to Change,* edited by F. Howe. New York: McGraw-Hill, Incorporated.

Robbins, L., and Kahn, E. D. 1985. "Sex Discrimination and Sex Equity for Faculty Women in the 1980s." *Journal of Social Issues* 41(4): 1-16.

Rodgers, F. S., and Rodgers, C. November–December 1989. "Business and the Facts of Family Life." *Harvard Business Review,* 212-29.

Rogan, H. 30 October 1984. "Executive Women Find it Difficult to

Balance Demands of Job and Home." *Wall Street Journal.* p. 33.

Rose, M. 1989. *Lives on the Boundary.* New York: Penguin Books.

Rosenfeld, R. A., and Jones, J. 1987. "Patterns and Effects of Geographic Mobility for Academic Women and Men." *Journal of Higher Education* 58(5): 493–515.

Rothblum, E. D. 1988. "Leaving the Ivory Tower: Factors Contributing to Women's Voluntary Resignation from Academia." *Frontiers* 10(2): 14–17.

Russell, S. H.; Cox, R. S.; and Williamson, C. 1990. *Institutional Policies and Practices Regarding Faculty in Higher Education 1988.* Washington, D.C.: U.S. Department of Education, Office of Education. ED 317 128 108 pp. MF–01; PC–05.

Russell, S. H.; Cox, R. S.; Williamson, C.; Boismier, J.; Javitz H.; and Fairweather, J. 1988. *Faculty in Higher Education Institutions.* Washington, D.C.: U.S. Department of Education, Office of Educational Research and Improvement. ED 321 628. 109 pp. MF–01; PC–09.

Sandler, B. 1981. "Strategies for Eliminating Sex Discrimination: Times that Try Men's Souls." In *Sex Discrimination in Higher Education,* edited by J. Farley. Ithaca: New York State School of Industrial Labor Relations, Cornell University.

Savage, D. G., and Gordon L. 10 January 1990. "Supreme Court Ends Secrecy in Tenure Dispute." *Los Angeles Times,* A10.

Schacter, J. 1989. "The Daddy Track." *Los Angeles Times Magazine* 5(40): 6–12+.

Schwartz, F. 1989. "Management Women and the New Facts of Life." *Harvard Business Review,* January-February 1989.

Seeborg, I. S. 1988. "Division of Labor in Two-career Faculty Households." A paper presented at the International Conference for Women in Higher Education, El Paso, Tex.

Sheinberg, R. 1988. "Parental Leave Policies of Large Firms." In *The Parental Leave Crisis,* edited by E. Zigler and M. Frank. New Haven: Yale University Press.

Shenitz, B. 10 June 1990. "The Grande Dame of Gay Liberation." *Los Angeles Time Magazine,* 20+.

Simeone, A. 1987. *Academic Women: Working towards Equality.* South Hadley, Mass.: Bergin & Garvey Publishers.

Sorcinelli, M. D., and Near, J. P. 1989. "Relations Between Work and Life away from Work among University Faculty." *Journal of Higher Education* 60(1): 59–81.

Stafford, S. G., and Spanier, G. B. 1990. "Recruiting the Dual-career Couple: The Family Employment Program." *Initiatives* 53(2): 37–44.

Staub, K. October 1987. "Level of Female Participation: An Overlooked Factor in Salary Differences among Faculty Disciplines?" A paper presented at the Annual Conference of the Southern Association for Institutional Research and Society for College and University Planning, New Orleans, La. ED 290 393. 28 pp. MF–01; PC–02.

Stecklein, J. E., and Lorenz, G. E. 1986. "Academic Women: Twenty-four Years of Progress?" *Liberal Education* 72(1): 63–71.

Stokes, J. M. 1984. "Organizational Barriers and Their Impact on Women, Research Report." Washington, D.C.: National Association for Women Deans, Administrators, and Counselors. ED 264 747. 50 pp. MF–01; PC–02.

Strober, M. H., and Quester, A. O. 1977. "The Earnings and Promotion of Women Faculty: Comment." *The American Economic Review* 67(2): 207–13.

Swerdlow, M. 1989. "Men's Accommodation to Women Entering a Nontraditional Occupation: A Case of Rapid Transit Operatives." *Gender and Society* 3(3): 373–87.

Tannen, D. 1990. *You Just Don't Understand: Women and Men in Conversation.* New York: William Morrow and Co.

"Tenure Rate for Men and Women." 29 March 1989. *Chronicle of Higher Education* 35(29): A17.

Thorner, P. M. 1989. "Toward Equity: Starting to Thaw the Chilly Campus Climate for Women." *Initiatives* 52(2): 1–7.

Trost, C. 10 January 1989. "Boss's Backing Vital to Family Benefits." *Wall Street Journal*. B1.

United States Congress. Senate Committee on Human Resources. *Report of the Hearings on the Pregnancy Disability Act of 1977* before the Subcommittee on Labor of the Committee on Human Resources. ——Cong.,——sess., 1977. Washington, D.C.: Government Printing Office.

University of Virginia. 1988. *Toward Equity: The Final Report of the Task Force on the Status of Women.* Charlottesville: University of Virginia.

University of Wisconsin. October 1988. Report of the Committee on Parental Leave Policy. Madison: University of Wisconsin.

Vetter, B. M., and Babco, E. L. 1987. *Professional Women and Minorities: A Manpower Data Resource Service.* Washington, D.C.: Commission on Professionals in Science and Technology.

Washington, V., and Harvey, W. 1989. *Affirmative Rhetoric, Negative Action: African-American and Hispanic Faculty at Predominantly White Institutions.* ASHE-ERIC Higher Education Research Report No.2. Washington, D.C.: School of Education and Human Development, The George Washington University. ED 316 075. 128 pp. MF–01; PC–06.

Watkins, B. 16 April 1986. "Major Recruiting Job for New Professors Seen Facing Academe." *Chronicle of Higher Education.* 32(7): 1+.

Weis, L. November-December 1985. "Progress but No Parity: Women in Higher Education." *Academe.* 71(6): 29–33.

Weishaar, M.; Chiaravalli, K.; and Jones, F. 1984. "Dual-career Couples in Higher Education." In *Strategies and Attitudes: Women in Edu-*

cational Administration, edited by P. Farrant. Washington, D.C.: National Association of Women Deans, Administrators, and Counselors. ED 285 439. 197 pp. MF–01; PC–not available.

White, A., and Hernandez, N. 1985. *Perceptions of Women and Men in Counselor Education about Writing for Publication.* ED 265 445. 15 pp. MF–01; PC–01.

Widom, C. S., and Burke, B. W. 1978. "Performance, Attitudes and Professional Socialization of Women in Academia." *Sex Roles* 4(4): 549–62.

Williams, J. D.; Williams, J. A.; Anderson, V. T.; and Roman, S. J. April 1987. "A Ten–year Study of Salary Differential by Sex through a Regression Methodology." A paper presented at the annual meeting of the American Educational Research Association, Washington, D.C. ED 287 344. 18 pp. MF–01; PC–01.

Wilson, D., and Doyle, K. O., Jr. 1976. "Student Ratings of Instruction." *Journal of Higher Education* 47(4): 465–69.

Winkler, K. 12 January 1981. "Women Historians Have Greater Access to Some Jobs but Remain Concentrated in Underpaid Ranks." *Chronicle of Higher Education.* 21(8): 8.

Witt, S. L., and Lourick, N. P. 1988. "Sources of Stress among Faculty: Gender Differences." *The Review of Higher Education* 11(13): 269–84.

Wohl, F. A. April–May 1989. Letter to the Editor. *Harvard Business Review.* 67(3): 183.

Yoder, J. D. 1985. "An Academic Woman as a Token: A Case Study." *Journal of Social Issues* 41(4): 61–72.

Yogev, S., and Vierra, A. 1983. "The State of Motherhood among Professional Women." *Sex Roles* 9(3): 391–96.

Young, M. M. 1978. "Sex Discrimination in Higher Education." *The Civil Liberties Review* 5(2): 41–43.

Yuker, H. E. 1984. *Faculty Workload: Research Theory and Interpretation.* ASHE-ERIC Higher Education Research Report No.10. Washington, D.C.: School of Education and Human Development, The George Washington University. ED 259 961. 120 pp. MF–01; PC–05.

Zuckerman, H. 1987. "Persistence and Change in the Career of Men and Women Scientists and Engineers: A Review of Current Research." In *Women: Their Underrepresentation and Career Differentials in Science and Engineering.* Washington, D.C.: National Research Council. ED 285 752. MF–01; PC–08.

INDEX

A

Academic stress factors, 49
Affirmative action, 7
American Association of University Professors, 24, 28, 34
American Federation of Teachers, 30
American History Association, 9
Amherst College
       benefit coverage, 59
Angel, Marina, 23, 25
AT&T employee survey, 50
Australia
       female faculty, 23

B

Barnard College
       faculty changes, 16
Boston University, 32
Business faculty recruitment, 3

C

California State University System, 3
California, University of, at Santa Barbara, 3
California, University of, 2, 11, 31
       law school, 32
       maternity leave, 58
       promotion rates, 14
Career expectations
       male/female differences, 28
       women, 27
Carnegie Foundation study, 28
Case studies
       female faculty, 61-68
       male faculty, 68-72
Child-rearing, 48
       issues, 76
Children
       effect on careers for women, 40-42
Chung, Connie, 43
Claremont Graduate School, 19
Collegiality, 27
Columbia University, 23
Committee on the Education and Employment of Women in Science
  and Engineering, 10
Community service
       faculty, 56
Consortium on Financing Higher Education, 2
Coordinating Committee for the Status of Women, 14

---

numbers, 12
sexual hostility, 25
stressors, 49
support system, 38
Female scientists
marriage and motherhood, 36

G

Gender discrimination, 9
Georgia, University of, 30
Glass ceiling, 14

H

Hiring practices
family responsive, 73
Hiring rate
faculty, 10
History departments
women faculty, 13
Hofstra Law School, 25
female faculty, 16

L

Language patterns
men and women, 26
Law schools
female faculty, 16

M

Male work/family conflicts, 50
Male/female behavior, 26
Mandatory retirement, 2
Market conditions and salaries, 28-29
Maryland, University of
tenure rates, 12
Maternal and paternal roles
social attitudes, 47
Maternity leave, 48, 74
policy, 74
policy implications, 57
"Matthew Effect", 15
Minnesota, University of, 31
parental leave, 58-59
women faculty, 11
Minorities on campus, 6
Minority faculty, 6-7
Mobility constraints on women, 46

Redlands, University of, 11
    faculty birth study, 58
Replacement rates
    faculty, 2
Research and publication, 55
Retirement of faculty, 1
Revolving door policy, 12
Robert Half International
    survey, 50
Role segregation
    families, 45

S

Salaries
    life cycle factors, 29
    sex discrimination, 29
Salary differences
    male/female faculty, 28
San Francisco State University, 2
Scholarly productivity
    men and women, 33
Scholarship
    male perspective, 18
Shared power in marriage, 46
Social activities
    female faculty, 23
Social reality
    perceptions, 27
Student evaluations
    sex differences, 21
Swift, Eleanor, 32

T

Teaching, 54
    effectiveness, 54
    evaluation, 18
Tennessee, University of (Chattanooga)
    faculty women perception of discrimination, 13
Tenure clock, 76
Tenure
    female chemists, 15
    female faculty, 15
Tenure system
    discrimination, 19
The Chronicle of Higher Education, 4
TIAA-CREF study, 2
Time as a source of conflict, 43

Tokenism
> effect on women, 26
> female faculty, 24

U

Universities
> commitment to families, 71-72
> structure, 53

University community, 51-52

University governance, 55

University professorships
> structure, 51

V

Virginia, University of, 9, 11
> status of women study, 45

Wisconsin, University of
> faculty birth study, 58
> gender differences study, 48

W

Woman's career value, 45

Women
> at Berkeley, 14-15
> doctorates, 5
> expected behavior, 27
> in the corporate world, 41
> on American campuses, 9

Women and careers
> commitment, 41

Women faculty
> retention, promotion, and tenure, 11-12

Women workers
> expectations, 42

Women's role on campus, 20-21

Work/family conflicts, 41

Y

Yeshiva University
> governance, 55

ASHE-ERIC HIGHER EDUCATION REPORTS

Since 1983, the Association for the Study of Higher Education (ASHE) and the Educational Resources Information Center (ERIC) Clearinghouse on Higher Education, a sponsored project of the School of Education and Human Development at The George Washington University, have cosponsored the *ASHE-ERIC Higher Education Report* series. The 1991 series is the twentieth overall and the third to be published by the School of Education and Human Development at the George Washington University.

Each monograph is the definitive analysis of a tough higher education problem, based on thorough research of pertinent literature and insitutional experiences. Topics are identified by a national survey. Noted practitioners and scholars are then commissioned to write the reports, with experts providing critical reviews of each manuscript before publication.

Eight monographs (10 before 1985) in the ASHE-ERIC Higher Education Report series are published each year and are available on individual and subscription basis. Subscription to eight issues is $90.00 annually; $70 to members of AAHE, AIR, or AERA; and $60 to ASHE members. All foreign subscribers must include an additional $10 per series year for postage.

To order single copies of existing reports, use the order form on the last page of this book. Regular prices, and special rates available to members of AAHE, AIR, AERA and ASHE, are as follows:

Series	Regular	Members
1990-91	$17.00	$12.75
1988-89	15.00	11.25
1985-87	10.00	7.50
1983-84	7.50	6.00
before 1983	6.50	5.00

Price includes book rate postage within the U.S. For foreign orders, please add $1.00 per book. Fast United Parcel Service available within the contiguous U.S. at $2.50 for each order under $50.00, and calculated at 5% of invoice total for orders $50.00 or above.

All orders under $45.00 must be prepaid. Make check payable to ASHE-ERIC. For Visa or MasterCard, include card number, expiration date and signature. A bulk discount of 10% is available on orders of 15 or more books (not applicable on subscriptions).

Address order to
    ASHE-ERIC Higher Education Reports
    The George Washington University
    1 Dupont Circle, Suite 630
    Washington, DC 20036
Or phone (202) 296-2597
    Write or call for a complete catalog of ASHE-ERIC Higher Education Reports.

1991 ASHE-ERIC Higher Education Reports

1. Active Learning: Creating Excitement in the Classroom
   Charles C. Bonwell and James A. Eison

1990 ASHE-ERIC Higher Education Reports

1. The Campus Green: Fund Raising in Higher Education
   Barbara E. Brittingham and Thomas R. Pezzullo

2. The Emeritus Professor: Old Rank - New Meaning
   James E. Mauch, Jack W. Birch, and Jack Matthews

3. "High Risk" Students in Higher Education: Future Trends
   Dionne J. Jones and Betty Collier Watson

4. Budgeting for Higher Education at the State Level: Enigma,
   Paradox, and Ritual
   Daniel T. Layzell and Jan W. Lyddon

5. Proprietary Schools: Programs, Policies, and Prospects
   John B. Lee and Jamie P. Merisotis

6. College Choice: Understanding Student Enrollment Behavior
   Michael B. Paulsen

7. Pursuing Diversity: Recruiting College Minority Students
   Barbara Astone and Elsa Nuñez-Wormack

8. Social Consciousness and Career Awareness: Emerging Link
   in Higher Education
   John S. Swift, Jr.

1989 ASHE-ERIC Higher Education Reports

1. Making Sense of Administrative Leadership: The 'L' Word in
   Higher Education
   Estela M. Bensimon, Anna Neumann, and Robert Birnbaum

2. Affirmative Rhetoric, Negative Action: African-American and
   Hispanic Faculty at Predominantly White Universities
   Valora Washington and William Harvey

3. Postsecondary Developmental Programs: A Traditional Agenda
   with New Imperatives
   Louise M. Tomlinson

4. The Old College Try: Balancing Athletics and Academics in
   Higher Education
   John R. Thelin and Lawrence L. Wiseman

5. The Challenge of Diversity: Involvement or Alienation in the
   Academy?
   Daryl G. Smith

6. Student Goals for College and Courses: A Missing Link in Assessing and Improving Academic Achievement
   Joan S. Stark, Kathleen M. Shaw, and Malcolm A. Lowther

7. The Student as Commuter: Developing a Comprehensive Institutional Response
   Barbara Jacoby

8. Renewing Civic Capacity: Preparing College Students for Service
and Citizenship
   Suzanne W. Morse

1988 ASHE-ERIC Higher Education Reports

1. The Invisible Tapestry: Culture in American Colleges and
Universities
   George D. Kuh and Elizabeth J. Whitt

2. Critical Thinking: Theory, Research, Practice, and Possibilities
   Joanne Gainen Kurfiss

3. Developing Academic Programs: The Climate for Innovation
   Daniel T. Seymour

4. Peer Teaching: To Teach is To Learn Twice
   Neal A. Whitman

5. Higher Education and State Governments: Renewed Partnership,
Cooperation, or Competition?
   Edward R. Hines

6. Entrepreneurship and Higher Education: Lessons for Colleges,
Universities, and Industry
   James S. Fairweather

7. Planning for Microcomputers in Higher Education: Strategies
for the Next Generation
   *Reynolds Ferrante, John Hayman, Mary Susan Carlson, and
   Harry Phillips*

8. The Challenge for Research in Higher Education: Harmonizing
Excellence and Utility
   Alan W. Lindsay and Ruth T. Neumann

1987 ASHE-ERIC Higher Education Reports

1. Incentive Early Retirement Programs for Faculty: Innovative
Responses to a Changing Environment
   Jay L. Chronister and Thomas R. Kepple, Jr.

2. Working Effectively with Trustees: Building Cooperative Campus
Leadership
   Barbara E. Taylor

3. Formal Recognition of Employer-Sponsored Instruction: Conflict
and Collegiality in Postsecondary Education
   Nancy S. Nash and Elizabeth M. Hawthorne

4. Learning Styles: Implications for Improving Educational Practices
   Charles S. Claxton and Patricia H. Murrell

5. Higher Education Leadership: Enhancing Skills through Professional Development Programs
   Sharon A. McDade

6. Higher Education and the Public Trust: Improving Stature in Colleges and Universities
   Richard L. Alfred and Julie Weissman

7. College Student Outcomes Assessment: A Talent Development Perspective
   Maryann Jacobi, Alexander Astin, and Frank Ayala, Jr.

8. Opportunity from Strength: Strategic Planning Clarified with Case Examples
   Robert G. Cope

1986 ASHE-ERIC Higher Education Reports

1. Post-tenure Faculty Evaluation: Threat or Opportunity?
   Christine M. Licata

2. Blue Ribbon Commissions and Higher Education: Changing Academe from the Outside
   Janet R. Johnson and Laurence R. Marcus

3. Responsive Professional Education: Balancing Outcomes and Opportunities
   Joan S. Stark, Malcolm A. Lowther, and Bonnie M.K. Hagerty

4. Increasing Students' Learning: A Faculty Guide to Reducing Stress among Students
   Neal A. Whitman, David C. Spendlove, and Claire H. Clark

5. Student Financial Aid and Women: Equity Dilemma?
   Mary Moran

6. The Master's Degree: Tradition, Diversity, Innovation
   Judith S. Glazer

7. The College, the Constitution, and the Consumer Student: Implications for Policy and Practice
   Robert M. Hendrickson and Annette Gibbs

8. Selecting College and University Personnel: The Quest and the Question
   Richard A. Kaplowitz

1985 ASHE-ERIC Higher Education Reports

1. Flexibility in Academic Staffing: Effective Policies and Practices
   Kenneth P. Mortimer, Marque Bagshaw, and Andrew T. Masland

2. Associations in Action: The Washington, D.C. Higher Education Community
   Harland G. Bloland

3. And on the Seventh Day: Faculty Consulting and Supplemental Income
   Carol M. Boyer and Darrell R. Lewis

4. Faculty Research Performance: Lessons from the Sciences and Social Sciences
   John W. Creswell

5. Academic Program Review: Institutional Approaches, Expectations, and Controversies
   Clifton F. Conrad and Richard F. Wilson

6. Students in Urban Settings: Achieving the Baccalaureate Degree
   Richard C. Richardson, Jr. and Louis W. Bender

7. Serving More Than Students: A Critical Need for College Student Personnel Services
   Peter H. Garland

8. Faculty Participation in Decision Making: Necessity or Luxury?
   Carol E. Floyd

1984 ASHE-ERIC Higher Education Reports

1. Adult Learning: State Policies and Institutional Practices
   K. Patricia Cross and Anne-Marie McCartan

2. Student Stress: Effects and Solutions
   Neal A. Whitman, David C. Spendlove, and Claire H. Clark

3. Part-time Faulty: Higher Education at a Crossroads
   Judith M. Gappa

4. Sex Discrimination Law in Higher Education: The Lessons of the Past Decade. ED 252 169.*
   J. Ralph Lindgren, Patti T. Ota, Perry A. Zirkel, and Nan Van Gieson

5. Faculty Freedoms and Institutional Accountability: Interactions and Conflicts
   Steven G. Olswang and Barbara A. Lee

6. The High Technology Connection: Academic/Industrial Cooperation for Economic Growth
   Lynn G. Johnson

7. Employee Educational Programs: Implications for Industry and Higher Education. ED 258 501.*
   Suzanne W. Morse

8. Academic Libraries: The Changing Knowledge Centers of Colleges and Universities
   Barbara B. Moran

9. Futures Research and the Strategic Planning Process: Implications for Higher Education
   James L. Morrison, William L. Renfro, and Wayne I. Boucher

10. Faculty Workload: Research, Theory, and Interpretation
    Harold E. Yuker

1983 ASHE-ERIC Higher Education Reports

1. The Path to Excellence: Quality Assurance in Higher Education
   Laurence R. Marcus, Anita O. Leone, and Edward D. Goldberg

2. Faculty Recruitment, Retention, and Fair Employment: Obligations and Opportunities
   John S. Waggaman

3. Meeting the Challenges: Developing Faculty Careers. ED 232 516.*
   Michael C.T. Brooks and Katherine L. German

4. Raising Academic Standards: A Guide to Learning Improvement
   Ruth Talbott Keimig

5. Serving Learners at a Distance: A Guide to Program Practices
   Charles E. Feasley

6. Competence, Admissions, and Articulation: Returning to the Basics in Higher Education
   Jean L. Preer

7. Public Service in Higher Education: Practices and Priorities
   Patricia H. Crosson

8. Academic Employment and Retrenchment: Judicial Review and Administrative Action
   Robert M. Hendrickson and Barbara A. Lee

9. Burnout: The New Academic Disease. ED 242 255.*
   Winifred Albizu Melendez and Rafael M. de Guzmán

10. Academic Workplace: New Demands, Heightened Tensions
    Ann E. Austin and Zelda F. Gamson

*Out-of-print. Available through EDRS. Call 1-800-443-ERIC.

ORDER FORM

Quantity   **Amount**

_____ Please begin my subscription to the 1991 *ASHE-ERIC Higher Education Reports* at $90.00, 33% off the cover price, starting with Report 1, 1990   _____

_____ Please send a complete set of the 1990 *ASHE-ERIC Higher Education Reports* at $80.00, 41% off the cover price.   _____

_____ Outside the U.S., add $10 per series for postage   _____

Individual reports are avilable at the following prices:

1990 and forward, $17.00	1983 and 1984, $7.50
1988 and 1989, $15.00	1982 and back, $6.50
1985 to 1987, $10.00	

Book rate postage within the U.S. is included. Outside U.S., please add $1 per book for postage. Fast U.P.S. shipping is available within the contiguous U.S. at $2.50 for each order under $50.00, and calculated at 5% of invoice total for orders $50.00 or above. All orders under $45 must be prepaid.

PLEASE SEND ME THE FOLLOWING REPORTS:

Quantity	Report No.	Year	Title	Amount

Subtotal:	
Foreign or UPS:	
Total Due:	

Please check one of the following:
- ☐ Check enclosed, payable to GWU-ERIC.
- ☐ Purchase order attached ($45.00 minimum).
- ☐ Charge my credit card indicated below:
  - ☐ Visa   ☐ MasterCard

Expiration Date _____

Name _____

Title _____

Institution _____

Address _____

City _____ State _____ Zip _____

Phone _____

Signature _____ Date _____

SEND ALL ORDERS TO:
ASHE-ERIC Higher Education Reports
The George Washington University
One Dupont Circle, Suite 630
Washington, DC 20036-1183
Phone: (202) 296-2597